cooking
for friends

cooking
for friends

stylish recipes with great flavour

RYLAND
PETERS
& SMALL

LONDON NEW YORK

Alastair Hendy

photography by David Loftus

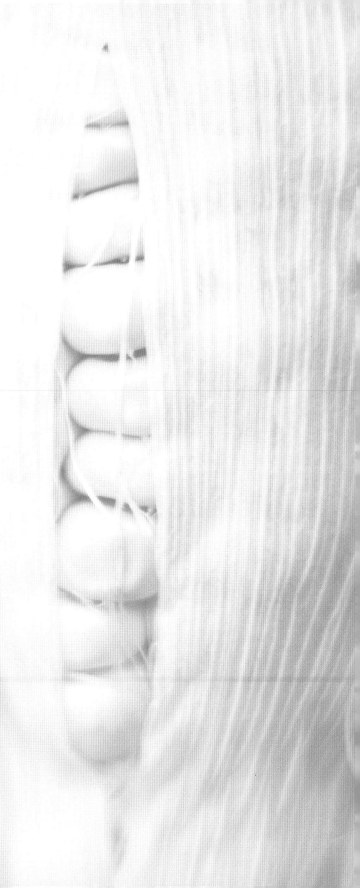

First published in Great Britain in 2000
by Ryland Peters & Small
Cavendish House,
51–55 Mortimer Street,
London W1N 7TD

10 9 8 7 6 5 4 3 2 1

Printed and bound in China by Toppan Printing Co.

ISBN 1 84172 068 2

A CIP record for this book is available from the British Library

Notes
All spoon measurements are level unless specified otherwise.
Ovens should be preheated to the specified temperature.
If using a fan-assisted oven, cooking times should be reduced
according to the manufacturer's instructions.
Specialist Asian ingredients are available in large supermarkets,
Thai, Chinese, Japanese and Vietnamese shops, as well as
Asian stores.

The material contained in this book was originally published in
Fresh in Spring, Fresh in Summer, Fresh in Autumn and Fresh
in Winter (published in 1999).

Designer
Robin Rout
Design Assistant
Suzanne Coetzee
Editors
Elsa Petersen-Schepelern
Maddalena Bastianelli
Production
Patricia Harrington
Art Director
Gabriella Le Grazie
Publishing Directors
Anne Ryland
Alison Starling

Stylist and
Food Stylist
Alastair Hendy
Cooking Assistant
Kate Habershon
Photographer's Assistant
Tara Fisher

To a dedicated cook,
my sister, Catherine

contents

introduction 7

soups and starters 8

vegetables 34

fish and seafood 68

chicken and other birds 92

meat 120

puddings 142

index 174

acknowledgements 176

Cooking is not just about the process of cooking. It's also about eating well, appreciating the ingredients and having a great time with friends. I can only be inspired to cook if I've got the right stuff to cook with: seasonal vegetables and fruit that are at their best, top-quality, fresh fish and meat from animals that have roamed about a bit and have had a happy life.

Buying fruit and vegetables in season is the key to good cooking. Not only are they less expensive and more easily available, they taste of what they are. Their flavours have not been lost through being forced out of season or by refrigeration during transport. Fresh from their native soil, you get their true garden flavours in full force. Cooking them couldn't be simpler, as you need do little to them. Cooking now is about spontaneity; a freedom to cook without getting bogged down with fiddly procedures. A bundle of this and a handful of that is the way I like to cook. No mucking about in the kitchen with complicated sauces or fretting too much over weights and measures. A knife, a chopping board and a couple of pans is generally all you need. Flavours are fresh and should be kept that way, so cooking times are short. Creating food is also about care and love, and sometimes involves extra time and attention, such as creating a good stock or slow-cooking a beautiful ham.

Throughout each chapter I've suggested variations on the dishes: different ways of combining parts of recipes with other ingredients; these are there to spark your own ideas. If one of the ingredients in a recipe isn't available when you do the shopping, rather than hunt high and low for it – which face it, most of us haven't got time for – buy something else you see that catches your eye and try it out. Enjoy your ingredients.

This book is for everyone – cooks and non-cooks, for those who are just starting out and for those who are looking for inspiration. If you're not an accomplished cook, just follow the recipes and all should be well. That's how I learnt to cook – from books. *Cooking for Friends* has short, quick recipes for when you want instant satisfaction, as well as others that need time in the oven. It's for everyone who loves food and entertaining.

I like to think there are no rules when it comes to serving food. Traditionally it's been three courses – starter, main and pudding – but nowadays, we tend not to worry too much with such formalities. After all, enjoying food is not about the order in which we eat it or how much we eat, it's more about what we eat. As long as what we eat tastes wonderful then that's what matters. One cooked course with some ripe cheese and a piece of fruit to follow can make a perfect meal. And without too much time spent fretting in the kitchen you'll be much more in the mood to enjoy it. My favourite way of eating is to sample a few different small courses – three starter-sized meze-like dishes to pick and nibble at – almost tapas style. When I'm eating out I find my fork strays into my friends' plates and, despite protestation from those who have chosen well, we usually all end up sharing everything. Eating is about sharing, enjoying good food with others, so why make it a course thing?

First courses can just as easily be turned into main courses. Often, too a first course could be all that you want but you need a little bit more of it. So just make more of it. Many of the recipes in this chapter can be treated as snacks or lunches, and the soups can easily be eaten as a meal in themselves with some warm crusty bread.

If you want to provide three courses, then a small bowl of soup to start is the answer. It can be made well in advance and you haven't got to fuss with it before serving. It's a simple option but if you want to make it more special, more of a meal, then add a few extra pre-prepared ingredients on serving: a bowl of thick pumpkin soup can be served with slices of goats' cheese and oven-baked pumpkin seeds; a clear Asian broth can have noodles, cooked shellfish or chicken and a smattering of fresh scented herbs strewn on top or a tomato and pepper soup can be served chilled with a spicy salsa. You can dress it up or keep it simple to fit your appetite or the occasion.

soups and starters

Asparagus soup with Asian greens

A clear, hot and sour Asian-style soup that's light and refreshing. The asparagus is lightly blanched to retain it's nutrients and *al dente* crispness. Add rice noodles and cooked prawns or chicken for a more substantial soup.

1.2 litres clear light chicken stock or 1 chicken stock cube dissolved in 1.2 litres hot water

1 tablespoon fish sauce*

3 teaspoons sugar

1 bird's eye chilli, finely sliced

3 cm fresh ginger or galangal, finely sliced

2 stalks lemongrass, trimmed and smashed with a rolling pin

1 teaspoon tamarind paste*

1 bundle young asparagus tips, sprue or wild asparagus

1 small bunch water spinach (*ong choi*), other Oriental leaves, baby spinach leaves or watercress, trimmed of any tough stems*

4 spring onions, chopped

juice of ½ lime

Crispy shallots (optional):

6 shallots, finely sliced

a pinch of salt

vegetable oil, for frying

Serves 6

Note: *Bottled fish sauce, tamarind paste and other Oriental ingredients such as water spinach and Chinese leaves are sold in Asian shops.*

1

Put the stock, fish sauce, sugar, chilli, ginger or galangal, lemongrass and tamarind paste in a saucepan, bring to the boil, reduce the heat and simmer for about 20 minutes.

2

Bring a large saucepan of salted water to the boil, plunge in the asparagus, return to the boil, simmer for 1 minute, then drain, rinse in cold water and transfer to a bowl of iced water.

3

To make the crispy shallots, if using, put in a bowl and toss with salt. Heat the vegetable oil in a heavy-based frying pan, add the shallots and sauté until dark brown and crisp.

4

Divide the blanched asparagus, water spinach and spring onions between 6 small soup bowls. Reheat the stock if necessary, add the lime juice, then strain over the ingredients in the bowls, top with the crispy shallots and serve.

Variations:

• Add other ingredients such as cooked prawns, poached chicken, wide rice noodles or tofu.

Chicken and butter leek soup

This is one of those antidote soups – cleansing, yet nourishing. Perfect for when you have overdone it and are hankering for something light but warm.

6 leeks

1 free-range chicken (about 1.5 kg)

2 carrots, halved

3 cm fresh ginger, peeled and thickly sliced

2 garlic cloves

2 teaspoons black peppercorns

1 fresh bouquet garni (3 fresh bay leaves tied together with large sprigs of parsley and tarragon)

60 g butter

1 tablespoon freshly squeezed lemon juice

a bunch of chives

salt and freshly ground black pepper

Serves 6

1

Slice 2 leeks in half lengthways and rinse thoroughly under running water to remove all the dirt. Cut the remaining leeks into thick rounds, rinse well and leave to soak in a bowl of cold water.

2

Put the chicken in a snug-fitting saucepan, add the halved leeks, carrots, ginger, garlic, peppercorns and bouquet garni and season generously. Cover with water, bring to the boil, skim off the froth, turn down the heat, cover and simmer gently for 45 minutes.

3

Turn off the heat and let the chicken cool completely in the stock.

4

When cold, remove the bird from the pan, flake the meat from the bone and discard the skin and bones*. Strain the stock and reserve.

5

Put the sliced leeks in a single layer across a wide saucepan. Season, add the butter and 125 ml of the stock. Heat to simmering, cover and gently poach for about 5 minutes or until the leeks are tender. Reheat the strained stock with the flaked chicken meat, add the lemon juice and spoon into bowls. Serve with the poached buttery leeks and a few chive stems.

__Note:__ If you want to make a richer stock, return the bones to the stock pot, cover and simmer for 1 hour more, then strain and discard the bones.

Variation:

• Omit the ginger, add broken pieces of pasta to the strained soup stock and cook as you reheat the chicken (a good way to use up all your dregs of pasta).

Pumpkin soup
with Creole roasted pumpkin seeds and goats' cheese

A bowl of hot pumpkin soup is just the boost you need on a cold day. Add a slice or three of goats' cheese and a good sprinkling of crisp pumpkin seeds and your soup will turn into a meal. Use dense-fleshed pumpkin with brown, grey or dark green skins – orange-skinned varieties tend to be watery.

1.5 kg pumpkin, halved and peeled

olive oil, for frying and baking

1 onion, finely chopped

2 garlic cloves, crushed

2 teaspoons cumin seeds, toasted

2 sprigs of thyme

2 bay leaves

½ teaspoon freshly grated nutmeg

1 teaspoon ground allspice

1.5 litres chicken stock

salt and freshly ground black pepper

1 goats' cheese log or 1 small tub of goats' curd cheese to serve

Creole roasted pumpkin seeds:

2 teaspoons olive oil

½ teaspoon garlic salt

½ teaspoon onion powder

1 teaspoon paprika

a pinch of cayenne

1 teaspoon dried oregano

Serves 6

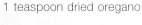

1

Remove and reserve the pumpkin seeds. Cut the pumpkin flesh into large chunks.

2

Heat 2 tablespoons olive oil in a deep frying pan, add the onion and garlic and fry until soft. Add salt and pepper, the cumin seeds, thyme, bay leaves, nutmeg and allspice. Fry for 1 minute. Add the stock and pumpkin and simmer gently for about 30 minutes or until soft. Purée in a food processor, transfer to a saucepan and keep it warm.

3

Clean the fibres off the pumpkin seeds, then toss the seeds with the olive oil, garlic salt, onion powder, paprika, cayenne and oregano. Spread over a baking sheet and roast in a preheated oven at 200ºC (400ºF) Gas 6 for 10–15 minutes.

4

Serve the soup accompanied by the toasted seeds and slices of goats' cheese.

Variations:

• Replace the toasted pumpkin seeds with fried crispy sage leaves.

• Use freshly grated Parmesan or Gruyère instead of goats' cheese.

Tomato and pepper soup

with aubergine croutons

It's important to use good, well-flavoured tomatoes for this soup – use Italian plum or the so called 'vine-ripened' varieties. Water is used instead of stock, to keep the flavours clean and sharp – perfect for the strict non-meat eaters.

6 large red peppers, preferably the long, tapered Italian variety

6 tablespoons olive oil

1 large onion, chopped

2 garlic cloves, halved

1.5 kg tomatoes, chopped

leaves and stalks from 8 sprigs of coriander (preferably with roots) or basil

a pinch of sugar

1 teaspoon Tabasco (optional)

1 aubergine, quartered lengthways, inner flesh discarded, flesh cut into small cubes

salt and freshly ground black pepper

Serves 6

1

Put the peppers directly on the gas flame. Turn every minute or so until blackened and blistered all over. Alternatively roast in a preheated oven at 220°C (425°F) Gas 7 for 20 minutes. Put them in a covered bowl and let cool. Scrape off the charred skin, then core and deseed the flesh.

2

Heat 2 tablespoons olive oil in a frying pan, add the onion and garlic and sauté until softened and transparent. Add the peppers, tomatoes, herb stalks, sugar, salt and pepper. Stew gently for 20 minutes, then add 600 ml water and stew for a further 20 minutes.

3

Sieve the mixture into a clean saucepan, pushing through all the flesh, and discarding the skins and seeds. Add the Tabasco, if using, warm through (but don't boil), then serve.

4

Season the aubergine then heat the remaining oil in the frying pan. Add the aubergine and fry until golden. Add to the bowls of soup and top with coriander or basil leaves.

Variations:

• Add chopped black olives and basil or avocado, or sautéed courgette, or even fried squid or feta cheese at the same time as the aubergine.

• Omit the peppers from the recipe and serve the soup chilled with a Bloody Mary salsa (chopped avocado, tomatoes and coriander, with grated red onion, lime juice and vodka).

Jerusalem artichoke chowder

with pan-seared scallops

Chowder (a thick white seafood soup flavoured with bacon) is traditionally thickened with potato. Using Jerusalem artichokes gives it a wintry earthiness, and the scallops elevate the humble soup to restaurant status. Jerusalem artichokes are not artichokes, but tubers like potatoes. These knobbly and earthy vegetables have a pronounced sweet flavour.

8 large scallops (without corals)

2 tablespoons olive oil

500 g Jerusalem artichokes

30 g butter

1 leek, white part only, rinsed and finely chopped

1 bay leaf

2 sprigs of thyme

3 potatoes, diced

3 slices smoked bacon

250 ml crème fraîche

300 ml milk

400 ml chicken stock

a squeeze of fresh lemon juice

salt and freshly ground black pepper

Serves 8 as a starter, 4 for supper

1

Trim the scallops if necessary and slice in half to make 16 rounds. Season, toss in the olive oil and set aside.

2

Peel and dice the Jerusalem artichokes and, as you do so, put them into a bowl of water acidulated with a dash of lemon juice, to prevent discoloration.

3

Heat the butter in a saucepan, add the leek, bay leaf and thyme and sauté until soft. Add the Jerusalem artichokes and potatoes, and cook for 1 minute more. Add the bacon, crème fraîche, milk, stock, lemon juice and seasoning. Bring to the boil, reduce the heat and simmer for 20 minutes or until soft.

4

Discard the bay leaf and bacon and, using a food processor or hand blender (which will give you a 'cappuccino' froth), blend to a smooth purée. Add extra stock or milk if it needs thinning, then taste and adjust the seasoning.

5

Heat a heavy-based frying pan until smoking hot and sear the scallops for 30 seconds on each side. Put the hot soup into bowls and add slices of seared scallop to each one.

Variation:

• Use freshly steamed cockles instead of scallops. Add them and their juices to the soup.

Spice island noodle soup
with dumplings

The spice islands of Indonesia still retain their plantations of nutmeg, clove, cinnamon and nuts. I dreamt up this recipe while sitting on top of an island volcano, looking over the spice groves below. It contains all these wonderful spice and nut flavours – trapped in a delicious dumpling.

1.5 litres light chicken stock

2 stalks lemongrass, trimmed and smashed

8 kaffir lime leaves, torn,
or the juice of ½ lime, plus 1 teaspoon sugar

2 garlic cloves, thickly sliced

3 cm fresh ginger, thickly sliced

1 packet rice vermicelli noodles, about 30 g, soaked in hot water for 4 minutes, drained and rinsed

Chinese leaves, such as bok choy

Spice dumplings:

250 g peeled prawns, fresh or frozen and thawed

250 g pork mince

3 cm fresh ginger, peeled and finely grated

2 tablespoons finely chopped coriander

60 g canned bamboo shoots, drained

16 macadamia nuts

4 spring onions, trimmed and chopped

2 small red chillies, finely chopped

½ tablespoon *kecap manis* or dark soy sauce

1 tablespoon fish sauce or 1 teaspoon salt

2 tablespoons lime juice

a pinch of ground cloves

a pinch of ground cinnamon

1 small egg, lightly beaten, to bind

vegetable oil, for frying

Serves 6

1

Put the chicken stock, lemongrass, lime leaves or juice and sugar, garlic and ginger in a saucepan, bring to the boil and simmer, covered, for about 20 minutes. Taste and add salt if necessary. Strain into a clean pan and discard the flavourings.

2

To make the dumplings, put the prawns in a food processor and chop for 1–2 seconds. Transfer to a bowl. Add all the remaining ingredients except the egg and oil to the processor and work to a coarse crumb consistency. Mix with the prawns and egg. Roll the mixture into walnut-sized balls and chill for 30 minutes.

3

Heat the vegetable oil in a frying pan or deep-fryer, add the dumplings in batches and cook gently until golden brown all over, about 2–3 minutes. Remove and set aside.

4

To serve, reheat the broth and arrange a portion of noodles and a few leaves in 6 deep soup bowls. Divide the dumplings between the bowls and pour over the hot lime broth.

Variations:

• Use Brazil nuts instead of macadamia nuts.

• Spear each dumpling with a bamboo skewer, fry and serve with drinks.

Asparagus brunch with prosciutto soldiers

The traditional way to cook asparagus is to stand the bundle upright in a tall saucepan and simmer in a few centimetres of water. However, you'll need a special pan: instead, simmer the spears in salted water for a few minutes in an ordinary pan, or steam in a metal or bamboo steamer.

6 hen's or duck eggs

1 bundle green asparagus (about 30 spears)

sea salt and cracked black pepper

butter, for brushing

Prosciutto soldiers:

6–12 slices white or brown bread, toasted

butter, for spreading

6–12 slices finely cut prosciutto ham

Serves 6

1

To cook soft-boiled eggs, prick the blunt ends to prevent cracking, put into a saucepan of cold water and bring to the boil. When the water reaches boiling point, set the timer for 4 minutes for hen's eggs, and 6 minutes for duck eggs. Put into egg cups set on 6 dinner plates.

2

To prepare the asparagus, steam for a few minutes (or simmer in salted water) until tender but still crisp – test with the point of a knife. Remove from the steamer, brush with melted butter and divide between the dinner plates.

3

To make the soldiers, toast the bread, spread with butter, trim the crusts and cut into 2–3 lengths. Wrap with prosciutto and add to the plates. Serve with sea salt and freshly ground black pepper.

4

To eat, dip the toasted soldiers and the asparagus tips into the egg.

Roasted tomatoes in herb oil

with char-grilled bread and baby mozzarella

I love it when restaurants give you a saucer of olive oil and balsamic vinegar plus bread and a few olives – just to keep your stomach occupied while you make a decision over the menu. It looks good, needs virtually no preparation, and tastes great – so why not do it at home. Keep it as simple as that, or add sliced tomato and a few basil leaves, or do a little extra preparation, and try this idea – dishes to dip into or pile on to grilled bread – a self-assembly toast. This barely needs a recipe.

12 small to medium tomatoes

2–4 tablespoons chopped herbs, such as basil, dill, parsley, oregano, marjoram and/or chives

2 tablespoons virgin olive oil

1 or 2 ciabatta loaves, sliced

1 fat garlic clove, halved

1 teaspoon balsamic vinegar

6 baby buffalo mozzarella or 1 buffalo mozzarella, cut into chunks

sea salt flakes and coarsely crushed black pepper

Serves 6

1

Roast the tomatoes in a preheated oven at 220°C (425°F) Gas 7 for about 8 minutes. Cool, peel and put in a bowl.

2

Mix the herbs with the oil, pour over the tomatoes and let stand for a few hours or overnight.

3

When ready to serve, grill the slices of bread on both sides then rub with the cut garlic clove. Put the sea salt and pepper in separate small dishes.

4

Drain the tomatoes and reserve the oil. Put the tomatoes in 1 small dish and strain the oil into another, adding a splash of balsamic vinegar. Add a small dish of the mozzarella.

5

Make up your own toast at the table, or eat the tomato and mozzarella separately and dip the toast in the balsamic oil.

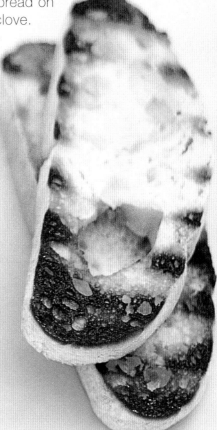

Variations:

• Add extra dishes, such as jars of vegetable antipasto and cured meats from a delicatessen.

• Serve other dishes such as salami, prosciutto, oven-roasted tomatoes (page 80), roasted vine tomatoes and bean salad (page 38) or char-grilled aubergine (page 126).

Green fruit gado gado

with lime and peanut dressing

Classic Indonesian gado gado is a salad of blanched shredded vegetables, cucumber and hard boiled eggs with a sweet, hot, peanut dressing. Unripe (known as green) papaya and mango are common to Asian salads – they're best when finely shredded and tenderized with heavily lime-juiced dressings.

100 g skinned unsalted peanuts, coarsely crushed

1 garlic clove

½ teaspoon salt

2 small red chillies, deseeded and chopped

80 g palm sugar or light muscovado sugar

4 limes

½ tablespoon caster sugar

selection of sour fruits, such as green (unripe) mango, green (unripe) papaya, starfruit or cucumber, peeled, pitted or deseeded, and shredded* as necessary

a handful of basil, coriander and mint leaves

Serves 6 as a first course

***Note:** A mandoline is the best tool for the job*

1

Dry-roast the crushed peanuts in a hot frying pan until toasted and flecked with brown all over.

2

Using a mortar and pestle, pound the garlic and salt until crushed to a purée. Add the chillies and pound until mashed. Pound in the sugar, then the toasted peanuts (if your mortar is full, do in batches). Don't grind all the peanuts to fine granules: some should remain coarsely crushed. Stir in the juice of 2 limes (use a little juice earlier if the mixture is too stiff to work).

3

Mix the caster sugar with the juice of 1 lime until dissolved. Toss the prepared fruits and herbs in the sweetened lime juice.

4

Cut the skin and pith from the remaining lime and slice out the segments from the surrounding membrane.

5

To assemble the salad, put small mounds of the sour fruit and herb salad on each dish (I use a 2-pronged carving fork to twist the salad like spaghetti). Top with the chilli peanut dressing and cover loosely with more salad and lime segments.

Variations:

• Eat the salad and peanut dressing wrapped up in lettuce leaves.

• Add freshly grated or shavings of coconut.

• Serve on banana petals with chopsticks – purple banana flowers are available from specialist Asian food shops.

Avocado and coriander toast

Avocado has to be the perfect food – convenient, delicious and good for you. The dark, warty-skinned Haas variety has the best flavour and texture. It goes well with many herbs, but coriander is especially good.

2 avocados, halved and pitted

juice of 1 lime, plus extra, for sprinkling

2 tablespoons virgin olive oil, plus extra for sprinkling

green jalapeño Tabasco sauce (or regular), to taste

4–8 slices bread, such as cornmeal, ciabatta or crusty farmhouse white

a bunch of coriander sprigs, thoroughly washed and drained, stems removed

sea salt and freshly cracked black pepper

Serves 4–6

Variations:

Pile higher with:

• Cooked prawns or crab marinated in sweetened lime juice.

• Poached chicken and toasted cumin seeds.

• Orange-scented olive oil, chopped spring onion and cherry tomatoes.

1

Using a teaspoon, scoop the avocado flesh into a food processor. Add the lime juice and 2 tablespoons of the olive oil, the Tabasco, salt and pepper. Process briefly. Alternatively, scoop the avocado with a teaspoon into a bowl, then add the dressing.

2

Char-grill or toast the bread on both sides and sprinkle with a little salt and extra oil.

3

Spread the avocado thickly over the toast, sprinkle with the remaining olive oil and lime juice, salt and pepper. Pile coriander on top.

Roasted mushrooms

with horseradish mascarpone

Mushrooms on toast are, for me, the definitive mushroom meal. Simple and straight to the point. Though I don't usually like to muck about with it, this recipe with hot horseradish and thyme still follows the purist path – the combination is wonderful.

6 large open mushrooms, stems removed, caps well brushed

a bunch of thyme

120 g butter, softened, plus extra, for greasing

3 garlic cloves, crushed

6 thick slices white bread, toasted

sea salt and freshly ground black pepper

Horseradish mascarpone:

5 cm fresh horseradish root, peeled and grated, or 2 tablespoons horseradish sauce

200 g mascarpone cheese

Serves 6

1

Thoroughly mix the freshly grated horseradish with the mascarpone and set aside.

2

Put the mushrooms, gills upward, in a greased roasting tin. Sprinkle with sea salt and pepper, and tuck the thyme around them.

3

Mix 90 g of the butter with the garlic and dot over the mushrooms. Roast in a preheated oven at 190°C (375°F) Gas 5 for about 10 minutes.

4

Spread the toast with the remaining butter. Add a mushroom and a spoonful of horseradish mascarpone to each slice. Sprinkle with the thyme leaves and serve.

Pea quiche

Classic quiche, with eggs, cream and salty bacon. You can't beat it! Add fresh cooked peas and nothing could be easier, or taste and look so good – one course in a slice. Serve plain, or top with more peas and a sprig of basil.

1 pack frozen shortcrust pastry, about 500 g, thawed

1 tablespoon olive oil

90 g pancetta or bacon lardons

1 garlic clove, finely chopped

350 g cooked green peas

1 tablespoon torn fresh tarragon or basil

4 free-range eggs, beaten (retain a spoonful for brushing the pastry)

200 ml double cream

sea salt and freshly ground black pepper

To serve (optional):

about 125 g shelled peas, cooked

sprigs of basil or mint

Serves 4–6

1

Roll out the pastry and use to line the base and sides of a deep 16 cm springform or loose-based cake tin. Prick the base of the pastry and chill.

2

Heat the oil in a frying pan, add the pancetta or bacon, fry until crisp, then stir in the garlic. Scatter the crispy mixture over the base of the pastry, fill the case with peas, then scatter with tarragon or basil.

3

Put the eggs, cream, salt and pepper in a bowl, beat well, then pour the mixture into the tart case. Brush the pastry with the reserved egg and cover loosely with foil.

4

Bake in a preheated oven at 200°C (400°F) Gas 6 for about 45 minutes or until set. Check after 20 minutes: if the top is browning, cover the top of the quiche with foil and move to the bottom shelf of the oven. Serve warm as is, or topped with a pile of peas and sprigs of basil or mint.

Variations:

• Use ricotta instead of cream, and add layers of blanched sliced courgettes.

Gone are the days when vegetables were just 'two veg' that sat alongside the meat, and gone too are the days when vegetables on their own, without meat, were for vegetarians only. With the globalization of our cooking and availability of world produce, we can now do so much more with our veg. I live on vegetables. Not because they're good for me but because I like eating them, they have such breadth and depth of flavour. I eat meat and fish too, but I wouldn't notice or feel I'd missed out somewhere if I'd had neither in a week.

For vegetables to be good, they must be fresh. That may sound a bit obvious, but so often we make do with what we are offered. Supermarket neatly packeted salad and perfectly boxed red tomatoes may look the part but how fresh are they? And what about flavour? If they are not in season then the chances are they've come a long way, from another part of the globe. They will not be as fresh as home grown and will lack the flavours we look for. Try and stick to vegetables that are in season and if you're not sure what comes when, here are a few pointers: they will be piled high because they're plentiful; they will look vibrant because they're brand spanking fresh; and should be about half the price they normally are because they're home grown. And that too explains why you should want them in the first place. They are the best. When I cook with vegetables, I like to try and keep them looking and tasting of what they are, only enhanced by what is added. The perfect food can be as simple as a plate of hothouse-warm sliced tomatoes annointed with good virgin oil; a dish of freshly pulled and boiled buttered root vegetables; or a bowl of mashed potato fragrant with saffron butter. All good enough to eat on their own. Take pleasure in the best. Look forward to, anticipate and relish the roots, stems and greens of the season – it makes cooking easy.

vegetables

Caesar greens

with gentlemen's relish toast

Use tender open-hearted greens or Italian cavolo nero (black cabbage) – a fine sweet cabbage that needs only the simplest of cooking. It is very good with anchovies and with this creamy Parmesan dressing and salty anchovy baked toasts. 'Eat up your greens' – happily.

mixed open-heart winter greens, cavolo nero, kale or sea kale, trimmed and tough stems removed

60 g fresh Parmesan cheese, finely grated

Gentlemen's relish toast:

butter, for spreading

1 baguette, thinly sliced diagonally

Gentlemen's Relish, for spreading (or 1 can anchovy fillets puréed with a dash of Worcestershire sauce)

Creamy dressing:

2 egg yolks

1 garlic clove, crushed

2 tablespoons sherry vinegar

200 ml olive oil

2 tablespoons single cream

sea salt and freshly ground black pepper

Serves 6

Variations:

• Finely slice the greens and toss into cooked pasta with the dressing, the Parmesan and finely chopped anchovy fillets.

• Dip veal escalopes in seasoned flour, then in beaten egg, then in breadcrumbs. Fry in butter on both sides. Add 4 finely chopped canned anchovies to the dressing. Serve the schnitzel with the Caesar greens.

1

To make the dressing, whisk the egg yolks in a bowl with the garlic, vinegar and seasoning. Whisk in the olive oil thoroughly, then the cream.

2

For the toasts, butter the baguette slices, arrange on a baking sheet and cook in a preheated oven at 190°C (375°F) Gas 5 until crisp. Spread thinly with Gentlemen's Relish.

3

Blanch the greens in boiling salted water for about 1 minute (sea kale will need 5 minutes). Drain and toss with the dressing and sprinkle heavily with the Parmesan. Serve the greens piled onto the toasts.

Roasted vine tomatoes

with cannellini bean salad and tapenade oil

Tomatoes grow on bushes, not vines, yet we call tomatoes sold on the stem 'vine tomatoes', probably because they look vaguely like a bunch of grapes. Roasted on their stems, they keep that just-picked look on the plate.

6 'vines' of baby tomatoes, about 6 fruit each

virgin olive oil, for brushing and dressing

800 g canned cannellini beans, rinsed and drained

1 medium red onion, finely chopped

2 garlic cloves, crushed

3 tablespoons coarsely chopped flat leaf parsley or torn basil leaves

2 tablespoon ready-made tapenade*

½ teaspoon sugar

juice of 1 lemon

sea salt and cracked black pepper

Serves 6

*Tapenade, or olive paste, is available in Italian delicatessens and larger supermarkets.

1

Arrange the tomato 'vines' in a single layer on a baking sheet, brush with olive oil and sprinkle with salt and pepper. Roast in a preheated oven at 220ºC (425ºF) Gas 7 for 6–8 minutes, until the skins have lightly blistered.

2

Put the beans, onion, garlic, parsley and tapenade in a bowl and stir gently. Dissolve the sugar in the lemon juice and add to the bean mixture. Stir in about 2 tablespoons olive oil and let stand at room temperature for 30 minutes.

3

To serve, spread the bean salad over serving plates, add a 'vine' of tomatoes to each plate, spoon over any remaining bean dressing and tomato roasting juices and dress liberally with more olive oil.

Variations:

• Make into a more substantial course by adding flakes of blackened salmon (page 80), roasted cod, fried mullet or barbecued monkfish kebabs.

• Give it the niçoise treatment and mix the tapenade with mayonnaise, add halved boiled eggs, anchovies and rare-roasted tuna.

Broad bean felafels with herb radish salad

Felafels are the pride of Lebanese cooking, starring favourite Middle Eastern herbs like mint, parsley and coriander. Don't be discouraged by the long list of ingredients – this recipe is very simple.

200 g podded broad beans

200 g chickpeas, soaked overnight in cold water to cover

3 garlic cloves, crushed

4 spring onions, chopped

1 heaped tablespoon chopped parsley

1 heaped tablespoon chopped coriander

1 heaped tablespoon chopped dill

1 heaped tablespoon chopped mint

3 teaspoons ground coriander

3 teaspoons ground cumin and 1 teaspoon cumin seeds, pan-toasted

3–4 tablespoons olive oil

1 tablespoon lemon juice

1 teaspoon baking powder mixed with 2 tablespoons warm water

2 tablespoons sesame seeds, pan-toasted

sea salt and freshly ground black pepper

6 warmed pitta breads, to serve (optional)

vegetable oil, for frying

1

Put the broad beans, chickpeas, garlic, spring onions, parsley, coriander, dill, mint, cumin, olive oil, lemon juice and baking powder mixture in a food processor and process to a coarse paste. Add salt and pepper to taste. Chill.

2

Roll the felafel mixture into walnut-sized balls. Roll one third of the balls in the plain sesame seeds and another third in the toasted sesame seeds. Leave the remainder plain. Heat the oil in a frying pan, saucepan or wok and gently shallow-fry or deep-fry the felafels until golden. Drain on crumpled kitchen paper.

3

To make the salad, put the yoghurt, lemon juice, tahini paste, salt and pepper in a bowl and beat with a fork. Add the salad leaves, herbs, cucumber and radish. Toss gently.

4

Serve the felafels with the salad on plates or in warm pitta bread.

Herb radish salad:

4 tablespoons plain yoghurt

1 teaspoon lemon juice

1 teaspoon tahini paste

assorted salad leaves and herbs, such as mizuna, golden orach, misome, mint and coriander

6 cm cucumber, finely sliced

6 radishes, finely sliced

sea salt and freshly ground black pepper

Serves 6

Tomato and pimiento tart

Pimientos are large, heart-shaped peppers (not to be confused with pimento or Jamaican allspice). If you can't find them, make this tart with tomatoes only (buy 2 punnets extra). Yoghurt cheese needs a bit of planning and this quantity of yoghurt makes more than you'll need for this tart– use it up on toast or with cheese biscuits. If you don't have time to make your own cheese, use Philadelphia cream cheese instead.

500 ml plain Greek yoghurt

1 teaspoon salt

1 large garlic clove, crushed

3 tablespoons finely chopped mixed fresh herbs, such as parsley, basil, chives, dill and tarragon, plus sprigs for serving

½ packet frozen puff pastry (210 g), thawed

1 punnet cherry tomatoes (about 20)

3 canned pimientos, or red peppers drained, deseeded and sliced lengthways

1 egg, lightly beaten, to glaze

Serves 6

Variations:

• Spread the pastry with a layer of tapenade and top with tomatoes.

• Cover with sliced tomatoes, bake and serve with fresh pesto.

• Flavour the yoghurt cheese with toasted cumin seeds, sprinkle with paprika and eat with toast.

1

Two days in advance, mix the yoghurt, salt and garlic in a small bowl or jug. Place a large square of muslin in a large bowl and pour in the yoghurt mixture. Gather up the corners and sides and tie tightly with string. Tie the bundle to a long-handled spoon and suspend over a deep container. Chill in the refrigerator for 2 days to allow the whey to drain from the yoghurt.

2

When ready to cook, discard the whey, put the yoghurt cheese into a bowl and mix in the chopped herbs.

3

Roll out the pastry to a rectangle or circle and spread with half the cheese, leaving a 1 cm border around the edges. Top with the whole baby tomatoes and strips of pimiento. Brush the edges of the pastry with beaten egg.

4

Bake in a preheated oven at 220°C (425°F) Gas 7 for 35 minutes or until the pastry has risen and is golden. Scatter with herbs and serve hot.

Asparagus filo tart with spinach and potato

Asparagus might have been specially made for the tart treatment – use long spears for a square tin or short ones for a tranche tin.

1 bundle asparagus, about 15 long spears or 20 short, ends trimmed

1 bunch spinach, about 20 large leaves, washed and trimmed

2 large potatoes, sliced

50 g butter, melted (reserve a tablespoon for glazing the pastry)

4–6 sheets filo pastry

175 g Gruyère, grated

½ teaspoon freshly grated nutmeg

3 eggs, lightly beaten

250 ml double cream

sea salt and freshly ground black pepper

olive oil, for poaching

To serve:

125 g Parmesan cheese, in the piece, shaved with a vegetable peeler

a small handful of chives

Serves 4

1

Plunge the asparagus into a pan of boiling water, remove immediately, drain and refresh in iced water. Drain. Pat dry with kitchen paper. Do the same with the spinach.

2

Put the potato slices in a saucepan, cover with olive oil, heat gently, then poach without browning until tender. Remove, then strain and reserve the oil for another use.

3

Brush a 23 cm square tin or 35 x 10 cm tranche tin with a little melted butter and line with a sheet of filo. Brush with more butter and top with another sheet of filo. Repeat until all the sheets are used. Trim the edges.

4

To assemble the tart, arrange a layer of cooked potato in the bottom of the pastry-lined tin. Season lightly with salt, pepper and nutmeg. Add a layer of spinach and season again. Add the Gruyère and a second layer of potatoes and spinach, seasoning each one.

5

Beat the eggs and cream in a jug or bowl, then pour over the potatoes and spinach. Arrange a line of cooked asparagus over the top of the tart. Brush the pastry with the reserved butter.

6

Bake in a preheated oven at 180°C (350°F) Gas 4 for 30–35 minutes. Half way through the cooking time, cover the asparagus, but not the pastry edge, with a sheet of foil or buttered baking parchment. When the centre of the tart is just set, remove it from the oven and serve with shavings of Parmesan and chives.

Summer lasagne

This isn't a regular baked lasagne: it's much lighter, like a dressed summer pasta – a light and fruity tomato salsa with courgette and basil, under a blanket of ricotta and pasta.

6 sprigs of basil

5 tablespoons fruity virgin olive oil

2 strips of lemon peel

2 strips of orange peel

500 g ripe red tomatoes, skinned, deseeded and chopped*

2 sun-dried tomato halves (in oil), very finely sliced

6 baby globe courgettes, halved, or 2 regular courgettes halved and thickly sliced and blanched in salted boiling water

350 g ricotta, at room temperature

20 sheets lasagne pasta, green or plain

salt and freshly ground black pepper

Serves 6

1

Remove the basil leaves from the stems and reserve. Tear half the leaves and keep the remainder whole. Warm the oil in a small saucepan with the basil stems and citrus peel. Remove and discard the stems and peel.

2

Add the tomatoes, sun-dried tomatoes, salt and pepper, then stir in the courgettes. Heat gently for about 1 minute. Stir in the chopped basil just before serving. Season the ricotta.

3

Cook the lasagne in a wide saucepan of salted boiling water until just soft – move and separate the sheets as they cook. (You will need 18 sheets, but some may tear or stick together.) Carefully drain the lasagne, then hang the sheets around the edges of the colander so they don't stick together.

4

To assemble the lasagne, make free-form layers of all the ingredients on each serving plate, dress with any remaining infused oil and sprinkle with salt and freshly ground pepper.

Note: Prick the tomatoes all over, put in a bowl and cover with boiling water for 2 minutes. Drain. The skins will slip off easily.

Variation:

• Use roasted vine cherry tomatoes instead of chopped tomatoes (page 38).

Aubergine mozzarella lasagne

This is a no-bake lasagne. All you have to do is pre-cook the pasta and vegetables (a few hours in advance, if you like), then quickly assemble all the components, reheat and serve – a sort of lasagne-in-a-hurry. Fresh and healthy, it looks as if you've spent hours on it.

3 garlic cloves, crushed

1 small bunch of basil, stems and leaves separated

100 ml olive oil

20 sheets lasagne pasta, fresh or dried

3 aubergines, sliced lengthways into 12 slices

2 tablespoons tapenade or sun-dried tomato paste

4 courgettes (yellow and/or green), thinly sliced lengthways

2 mozzarella (preferably buffalo), thinly sliced

salt and freshly ground black pepper

Serves 6

1

Put the garlic, basil stems and olive oil in a saucepan and warm through for about 10 minutes to infuse the flavours.

2

Cook the lasagne in a wide saucepan of salted boiling water until just soft – move and separate the sheets as they cook. (You will need 18 sheets, but some may tear or stick together.) Carefully drain the lasagne, then put it into cold water to stop it overcooking or sticking together. Hang the sheets around the edges of the colander so they don't stick together.

3

Brush the aubergine and courgette slices on both sides with some of the infused oil. Cook in a preheated stove-top grill pan or frying pan, turning halfway through cooking, until seared and soft.

4

To assemble, arrange 6 slices of aubergine across a baking sheet. Top each slice with a sheet of lasagne, spread a little tapenade or tomato paste on each, then add a slice of courgette and mozzarella, and a couple of basil leaves. Repeat with all the ingredients, until you have 6 multi-storey piles of pasta, vegetables and mozzarella. Brush all over with more of the infused oil, cover loosely with foil and heat through in a preheated oven at 220°C (425°F) Gas 7 for about 5 minutes or until the cheese begins to melt.

Variations:

• Use oven-dried tomatoes (page 80) instead of sun-dried tomato paste. Alternative layering ingredients include seared aubergine, goats' cheese, Parma ham and basil; soft cheese, toasted pine nuts, cumin seeds, roasted red peppers and mint.

Spinach gnocchi with basil oil

Gnocchi are wonderful made with spinach or with a mixture of other leaves, such as rocket and sorrel. I've also made them with wild greens, including young nettle tops (don't worry – the sting is eradicated as soon as the leaves hit hot water). Usually, gnocchi are made by rolling pieces of dough off the end of a fork – this version is much easier.

150 g baby spinach, well washed

400 g ricotta, drained of excess whey

3 egg yolks

a pinch of ground allspice

30 g fresh Parmesan cheese, grated

1 tablespoon plain flour

2 tablespoons semolina

salt and freshly ground black pepper

Basil oil:

a small bunch of basil, coarsely chopped

6 tablespoons fruity virgin olive oil

Serves 6

1

To blanch the spinach, plunge into boiling salted water for 2 minutes. Drain, squeeze dry in a cloth, and chop very finely.

2

Put in a bowl with the ricotta, eggs, allspice, Parmesan, flour, semolina, salt and pepper. Work to a firm dough, adding extra flour if necessary.

3

Roll the dough into a long sausage shape, 2 cm thick. Cut into segments about 2 cm long and put on a lightly floured surface.

4

Mix the basil and oil in a small jug.

5

Bring a large saucepan of salted water to the boil, add the prepared gnocchi and cook for about 2–3 minutes until they rise to the top. Drain, divide between 6 heated plates or bowls and dress with the basil oil and black pepper.

Indian coconut dhaal

with peas and paneer

This soupy pea dhaal, or lentil stew, is made with coconut milk and paneer, the delicious North Indian curd cheese – use mozzarella if you can't find it. This recipe tastes even better if made the day before, so the flavour of the chillies, leaves and spices fully penetrate the split peas and cheese.

75 g yellow split peas, or channa dhaal, washed in several changes of cold water

2 teaspoons ground coriander

2 teaspoons cumin seeds

1 teaspoon fenugreek seeds

2.5 cm cinnamon stick

4 small dried chillies

6 small shallots, sliced

1 teaspoon ground turmeric

2 sprigs curry leaves*

200 g shelled green peas

400 ml coconut milk

250 g paneer cheese* or mozzarella, cubed

1 teaspoon mustard seeds

sea salt and freshly ground black pepper

vegetable oil, for frying

To serve:

1 packet pappadams

hot paprika, to sprinkle

Serves 4–6

Note: Available from Asian stores.

1

Put the yellow split peas in a saucepan with 600 ml water, bring to the boil, reduce the heat and simmer for about 50 minutes, skimming off the foam from time to time.

2

Grind the coriander, cumin, fenugreek, cinnamon and 1 dried chilli in a spice mill or coffee grinder. Heat 2 tablespoons of the oil in a frying pan, add the shallots and fry until soft. Stir in the ground spice mixture and the turmeric and fry until the shallots are golden-brown.

3

Transfer to the saucepan of split pea dhaal, add 1 sprig of curry leaves, season well and simmer for 10 minutes. Stir in the peas, coconut milk and paneer, then gently simmer the dhaal for 15 minutes – add extra water if the mixture has thickened too much (it should remain soupy).

4

Heat 2 tablespoons of the vegetable oil in a small frying pan, add the mustard seeds, the remaining chillies and curry leaves and fry for a few seconds. Add to the dhaal and serve in 1 large bowl or divide between 4 or 6 small bowls.

5

Wipe out the small pan, pour in 2 cm depth of the vegetable oil and heat until a small piece of pappadam or bread browns in 30 seconds. Fry the pappadams, one by one, until crisp. Remove, drain, sprinkle with hot paprika and serve with the dhaal.

Corn and sweet potato bhajia

with sambal dip

Don't be put off by the long list of ingredients – everything is easily put together. The sambal is not compulsory, but it is the business: it contains all the flavours of Indonesian cooking, salt, hot, sour and sweet, all in one dip. If you don't have time, serve the bhajia (plural of bhaji) with soy sauce instead.

3 fresh corn cobs

1 large sweet potato, finely sliced or grated

100 g flour

12 spring onions, finely sliced lengthways

4 small shallots, finely sliced

3 tablespoons chopped fresh coriander

3 cm fresh ginger, grated

1 garlic clove, crushed

2 small red chillies

1 teaspoon sugar

vegetable oil, for frying

Sambal dip:

1 stalk lemongrass, trimmed and finely chopped

1 garlic clove, crushed

3 red chillies, finely sliced

1 teaspoon shrimp paste (*blachan*), (optional)

1 tablespoon peanut oil

3 teaspoons caster sugar

4 tomatoes, deseeded and chopped

2 tablespoons *kecap manis* (Indonesian ketchup) or dark soy sauce

1 tablespoon tamarind paste mixed with 3 tablespoons water or 2 tablespoons lime juice with 2 tablespoons water

1 tablespoon crushed toasted peanuts, to serve (optional)

Serves 6

1

To make the sambal, mix the lemongrass, garlic, chillies and shrimp paste and fry in the peanut oil for about 1 minute. Stir in the remaining ingredients and let cool. Serve in a small dish, sprinkled with crushed toasted peanuts, if using.

2

Meanwhile, to make the bhajia, first cook the corn in a large saucepan of boiling water for 8 minutes. Drain, then hold the corn vertically on a board and slice off the kernels. Discard the core.

3

Mix the corn, sweet potato, flour, shallots, spring onions, coriander, ginger, garlic, chillies and sugar in a bowl. Add 100 ml warm water and stir to form a thick batter.

4

Heat the oil in a large frying pan, add tablespoons of the mixture and fry in small batches until golden on both sides. Serve the bhajia with the sambal.

Green tomato and basil curry

This is a Thai, soup-like curry. The sharpness of the tart green tomatoes is perfect with the sweet and salt flavours of the curry. If green tomatoes are unavailable, use underipe ones instead, adding them to the pan about 5 minutes before the end of cooking.

750 g green tomatoes, quartered

a handful of basil leaves, chopped, plus extra for serving

5 tablespoons virgin olive oil

600 ml canned coconut milk

1 tablespoon fish sauce

2 teaspoons sugar

salt and freshly ground black pepper

Curry paste:

4 large mild green chillies, chopped

5 hot green chillies, chopped

5 shallots, chopped

5 garlic cloves

3 cm ginger, chopped

1 stalk lemongrass, trimmed, outer casing discarded, chopped

6 kaffir lime leaves, finely chopped, or 1 teaspoon finely chopped lime zest

2 teaspoons shrimp paste (*blachan*), or anchovy essence

Serves 4–6

*****Note:*** *Shrimp paste is a salty Indonesian seasoning. If unavailable, omit it or use anchovy essence instead.*

1

Put all the ingredients for the curry paste into a food processor or blender and work to a paste. Add 2 of the quartered tomatoes and purée again.

2

Mix the chopped basil in a bowl with 3 tablespoons of the olive oil.

3

Heat the remaining oil in a wok or wide, shallow saucepan, add the paste and stir-fry until the oil separates – about 4 minutes.

4

Add the coconut milk, fish sauce, sugar, salt, pepper and 400 ml water. Bring to the boil, reduce the heat and simmer for about 15 minutes. Add the tomato quarters and gently simmer for a further 10 minutes. Stir in the basil-flavoured oil and serve with whole basil leaves on top – and plenty of plain boiled rice.

Variations:

• Before serving, you could stir in some fresh pesto, made without Parmesan – the creamy pine nuts add an extra dimension to the taste and texture, not dissimilar to the crushed nuts used in many Asian curry pastes.

• Add thin strips of stir-fried beef or chicken and other vegetables, such as Thai wing beans or dwarf beans. Use coriander instead of basil.

• Make a red tomato curry using red tomato and red chillies instead of green, adding whole cherry tomatoes 5 minutes before the end of cooking.

Pumpkin coconut curry

Make this curry with ordinary pumpkin, or with spaghetti squash – melon-shaped, with yellow flesh that pulls into strands when cooked. I prefer to bake it first before adding to the curry, to retain the long strands.

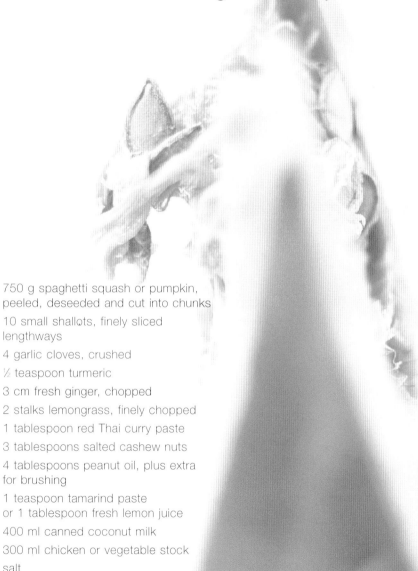

750 g spaghetti squash or pumpkin, peeled, deseeded and cut into chunks

10 small shallots, finely sliced lengthways

4 garlic cloves, crushed

½ teaspoon turmeric

3 cm fresh ginger, chopped

2 stalks lemongrass, finely chopped

1 tablespoon red Thai curry paste

3 tablespoons salted cashew nuts

4 tablespoons peanut oil, plus extra for brushing

1 teaspoon tamarind paste
or 1 tablespoon fresh lemon juice

400 ml canned coconut milk

300 ml chicken or vegetable stock

salt

to serve:

fresh coriander leaves

fresh beansprouts

Serves 6

1

If using spaghetti squash, brush it with a little oil and salt, then bake in a preheated oven at 190°C (375°F) Gas 5 for 30–45 minutes until cooked. Pull the flesh into strings. If using regular pumpkin, cut it into bite-sized chunks.

2

Place 4 shallots, the garlic, turmeric, ginger, lemongrass, Thai curry paste and cashew nuts into an electric blender and process to a coarse paste.

3

Heat 2 tablespoons of the oil in a frying pan, add the paste and fry until it darkens, adding a drop more oil if required. Add the tamarind or lemon juice, pumpkin or squash, coconut milk and stock and simmer for 10 minutes or until the pumpkin is tender.

4

Heat the remaining oil in a second pan, add the remaining shallots and fry until crisp. Spread out on kitchen paper to drain. Sprinkle liberally with salt.

5

Divide the pumpkin or squash between 6 bowls and serve topped with fried shallots, coriander and beansprouts.

Indian spiced aubergine

with egg, basil and cardamom rice

The aubergine takes on a mildly spiced sweet and sour flavour. Eat it hot or cold (it's wonderful either way) or serve with freshly baked focaccia instead of rice, and you have great picnic food. Cook ahead, if you can, and leave for a few hours for the flavours to develop and meld. Reheat before serving.

3 cm fresh ginger, chopped

6 garlic cloves

1 onion, chopped

3 medium aubergines, quartered lengthways, with the central 'seed' core removed

125 ml mustard oil, peanut or corn oil, for frying, plus 1 tablespoon for sautéing

2 teaspoons ground cumin

2 teaspoons lightly crushed coriander seeds

3 teaspoons panchphoran spice mix*

a pinch of cayenne pepper

4 tomatoes, chopped

3 tablespoons red wine vinegar

4 teaspoons jaggery or muscovado sugar

a handful of fresh basil leaves

8 cardamom pods

300 g basmati rice

salt and freshly ground black pepper

4 hard-boiled eggs, peeled and halved, to serve

Serves 6

1

Put the ginger, garlic and onion in a food processor and work to a coarse paste.

2

Sprinkle the aubergine with salt and pepper. Heat 125 ml of the oil in a frying pan, add half the cumin and coriander seeds and the aubergine. Fry on all sides until lightly golden. Put the aubergine in a colander over a bowl.

3

Tip any collected oil from the aubergine back into the frying pan, heat and add the panchphoran. Fry for a few seconds until the seeds pop. Add the ginger paste, cayenne and the remaining cumin and coriander seeds and fry until the oil separates from the mixture, (adding extra oil if necessary). Add the tomatoes, vinegar and sugar and cook gently for about 10 minutes, stirring occasionally to prevent sticking.

4

Add the fried aubergine to the mixture and cook for a further 5–10 minutes. Add salt and pepper to taste. Keep hot and stir in half the basil just before serving.

5

Heat 1 tablespoon of oil in a deep saucepan, add the cardamom pods and sauté until aromatic. Add the rice and stir to coat the grains with oil. Add salt and 750 ml water, cover and bring to the boil. Reduce the heat and simmer very gently for 8 minutes. Turn off the heat and leave covered for 10 minutes.

6

Spoon the rice into 6 heated bowls, then top with the aubergines, the remaining basil and the halved, hard-boiled eggs.

Variations:

• Use fresh coriander or mint instead of basil.

• Add fresh curry leaves to flavour the curry or along with the cardamom to flavour the rice.

• Serve the spiced aubergine with pappadams instead of rice or stir a spoonful of melted creamed coconut into the rice just before serving.

Note: Panchphoran is available from Indian shops. If you can't find it, make your own: mix 2 teaspoons each of black mustard seeds, cumin seeds, nigella (onion) seeds, fennel seeds and fenugreek seeds – it's not imperative that you include all of these, but 'panch' means 'five'.

Pot-roasted red onions

with feta cheese and oregano

Peeled red onions are slow-baked with oregano and olive oil, then served with crumbled feta cheese. I'm not a big fan of quartered roast onions – they over-caramelize and taste too burnt at the edges. Baking or roasting them whole keeps them succulent and makes the bulbs meltingly tender, full of onion concentrate. You can swap oregano for rosemary, and you can take it even further if you like – see the variations below.

12 small or 6 medium red onions

2 teaspoons dried oregano

4 tablespoons olive oil

12 black olives

leaves from 4 sprigs of oregano

250 g feta or blue cheese, crumbled

sea salt and freshly ground black pepper

Serves 6

1

Stand the peeled onions in a snug-fitting casserole (with lid) or a roasting tin (use foil as a cover). Sprinkle with dried oregano, spoon over half of the oil and season generously. Cover and roast in a preheated oven at 180°C (350°F) Gas 4 for 45–60 minutes or until tender.

2

Remove the lid, put in the olives and a few of the fresh oregano leaves, baste with the remaining olive oil and return to the oven for 5 minutes. Serve with crumbled feta or blue cheese and the remaining oregano leaves.

Variations:

• Slice the roasted onions into quarters before serving and toss with all the ingredients, plus winter salad leaves, walnuts, a dash of walnut oil and balsamic vinegar.

• Cut in half lengthways and put cut side up in a gratin dish. Baste with garlic-infused olive oil and herbs, then lightly caramelize under a hot grill. Serve with mashed sweet potato and grilled lamb cutlets or pork chops.

Thyme buttered baby roots
with home-made horseradish cream

This dish of perfectly cooked tender little roots – tails, tops and all – is good enough as a course on its own. You can also use grown-up roots, cut to size. Hamburg parsley tastes and looks like baby parsnip, but has a more earthy herby flavour. Salsify is a long narrow hairy root, not the most endearing of objects, but with delicious creamy flesh.

45 g butter

4 sprigs of thyme

sea salt and freshly ground black pepper

Baby roots: a selection of:

baby waxy potatoes, unpeeled but scrubbed

baby carrots, unpeeled, trimmed and scrubbed

baby turnips, scrubbed, or large ones, peeled

Hamburg parsley root, peeled

salsify or scorzonera, peeled*

swede, peeled and cut into chunks

small parsnips, peeled

Jerusalem artichokes, peeled and cut into chunks*

Home-made horseradish and garlic cream (optional):

5 tablespoons crème fraîche

1 tablespoon freshly grated horseradish root

2 shallots, finely chopped

2 garlic cloves, crushed

2 tablespoons white wine vinegar

salt and freshly ground black pepper

Serves 6

__Note:__ Peeled salsify and Jerusalem artichokes should be put into a bowl of acidulated water (water with a dash of lemon juice) to prevent browning. Dip in the lemon water as you peel: it will stop your hands from staining too.

1
Put all the horseradish cream ingredients in a bowl and beat well. Taste and add a dash more vinegar or seasoning if necessary.

2
Melt the butter and strip the thyme leaves from their stems into the butter and leave to infuse while you cook the roots.

3
Simmer the prepared roots in salted water until cooked (pierce a large one with a knife to test). If certain roots are larger or thicker than others (such as parsnips), start off with them first, and cook for about 8 minutes, then add the smaller, narrower ones (such as baby carrots) and let simmer for a further 3 minutes. Drain and toss with the thyme butter, sea salt and black pepper. Serve with a spoonful of horseradish cream, if using.

Variations:

• Serve thyme buttered roots with:

• Salt beef (poached until tender with carrots, onion, bay leaf and peppercorns) and freshly grated horseradish.

• Beetroot aioli (mayonnaise mixed with crushed garlic and cooked puréed beetroot).

• Clay Pot Lemon Poussin (page 104).

• Roast rib of beef (include the horseradish and garlic cream) or with other roasted meats.

Porcini pizza with garlic butter

Porcini – 'little pigs' in Italian – are also known as ceps and are the kings of the mushroom family. Their flavour is rich and intense – the very essence of mushroominess. Don't make this with dried porcini, which should only be used in sauces, stocks and braises. Use other wild mushrooms instead.

125 g butter

400 g fresh porcini, sliced, or other wild mushrooms, wiped clean and woody stem ends removed

3 garlic cloves, crushed

2 mozzarella, thinly sliced

3 sprigs of rosemary

salt and freshly ground black pepper

Pizza dough:

15 g fresh yeast

500 g *typo 00* flour

1 teaspoon salt

a pinch of sugar

fine semolina, for dusting

Makes 4 or 12 pizzette

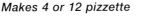

1

To make the pizza dough, dissolve the yeast in 250 ml warm water. Pile the flour on a work surface and make a well in the centre. Add the yeast mixture, salt and sugar. Mix to a soft dough, then knead until silky and elastic. Dust with flour, put in a bowl, cover and leave in a warm place for about 1 hour until doubled in size.

2

To make the topping, heat the butter in a wide frying pan, add the sliced porcini and fry briefly on both sides. Stir in the garlic and seasoning and remove from the heat. Heat a lightly oiled, heavy baking sheet in the oven, set at its highest setting, until very hot.

3

Knock back the risen dough with your knuckles and divide into 4 or 12 pieces. Flatten each with a rolling pin and, using your fingers (or rolling pin), stretch into long flat oval shapes. Dust on both sides with semolina. Brush with the garlic butter, scatter with slices of mozzarella and top with the porcini and the leaves from the sprigs of rosemary. Arrange on the preheated baking sheet and bake at the same temperature for 10–15 minutes for large or 8 minutes for small.

We're still a little afraid when it comes to cooking fish. And at the fish counter many of us are unsure of what to ask for. For some, it's difficult to imagine how to transform a complete fish – head, fins, tail and all – into four elegant portions on the dinner table. But don't be embarrassed to ask any questions you like – a lot of people in the queue behind you haven't much of a clue either.

If you like fish, you really like it, as I do. A fresh fish rubbed with seasoning, herbs and olive oil, and seared until crisp on the outside and just cooked within tastes fantastic. It's also very good for you and takes minutes to cook, which makes it my kind of food. But it has to be very fresh. So when picking out your fish look for bright clear eyes and blood-free, pink gills and ask the fishmonger when it was caught.

There is one snag with fish and that's the bones. If there's one thing that can put us off eating fish, it must be the idea of all those fiddly little bones to deal with. But there's a way out of this – buy fillets of fish. If the fish counter has no filleted fish then don't hesitate to ask for a whole fish to be cleaned and filleted for you. A sinch to prepare, as fast as a burger to cook – and 100% better for you – and the big plus, no bones. Just rub, crust, bathe or wrap, then sear, grill or roast.

Freshness is all-important for shellfish too. When it comes to mussels, cockles and clams, always throw out ones that remain open after you have scrubbed them. Then discard any that remain closed after they have been cooked. If you are cooking from fresh, all crustacea (excluding prawns), including lobsters and crabs should be live.

fish and seafood

Chilli crisp prawns and garlic chives with wasabi mayonnaise

Maybe I'm unusual in my desire to eat prawns unpeeled, but their shells turn crispy when blistered and take on the caramelized lime and chilli-garlic flavours in the pan. Garlic chives taste faintly spicy with a garlic-onion flavour. You can also use ordinary chives, spring onions or wild garlic leaves.

3–4 teaspoons wasabi paste*

6 tablespoons mayonnaise

12 whole uncooked king prawns

2 stalks lemongrass, trimmed, outer layers discarded, inside layers finely sliced

1 teaspoon chilli flakes

2 garlic cloves, chopped

1 tablespoon fish sauce

2 teaspoons sugar

2 tablespoons lime juice, preferably from kaffir limes

2 teaspoons grated lime zest

1 bunch Chinese garlic chives, some finely scissor-snipped, others left whole

sea salt

corn or peanut oil, for frying

Serves 6

*Note: Wasabi paste (hot Japanese horseradish) is sold in tubes, bottles or powder form in larger supermarkets and Asian shops.

1

Beat the wasabi and mayonnaise together. Spoon into small dishes.

2

Put the prawns in a bowl, add the lemongrass, chilli flakes, garlic, fish sauce, sugar, lime juice and zest. Mix well.

3

Heat 1 tablespoon of the oil in a heavy-based frying pan, add the prawns and scatter generously with sea salt. Sear on both sides until the shells are caramelized and brittle and the flesh opaque.

4

Toss the snipped chives with the prawns and serve on a bed of whole garlic chives.

5

To eat, remove the head and legs, dip the prawns into the wasabi mayonnaise and eat them whole, including the crispy shells.

Variations:

Chilli crisp prawns also go with:

• Noodles and extra chopped garlic chives.

• Stir-fried greens and extra garlic chives.

• Salad leaves.

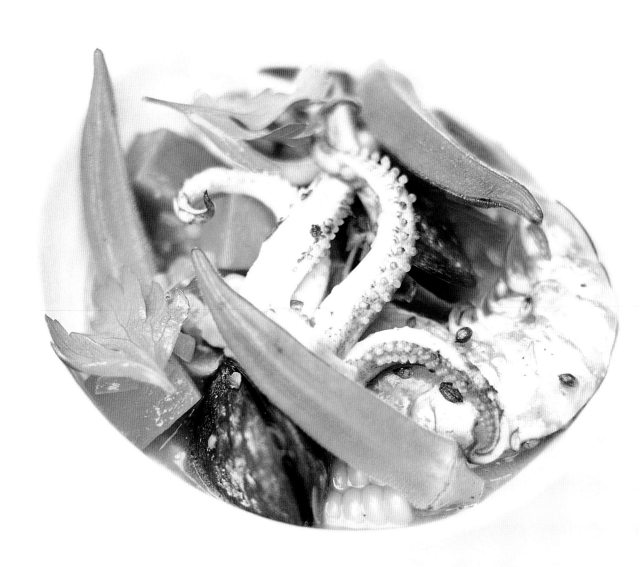

Seafood and corn gumbo

Gumbo is the Louisiana classic thickened with filé (ground sassafras leaves) or chopped okra and usually made with seafood, although chicken, duck and boudin sausage can be used too. My version is more like a *marinière* (no self-respecting Louisiana cook would add wine) – but it tastes brilliant anyway.

1 kg mixed seafood, such as mussels or clams, lobster, prawns or squid

2 fresh corn cobs

4 tablespoons olive oil

1 teaspoon chilli flakes

4 garlic cloves, crushed

4 shallots, chopped

3 carrots, diced

2 teaspoons coriander seeds

300 ml white wine

600 ml chicken stock

juice of 1 lime

a pinch of saffron

6 tomatoes, quartered

250 g okra

2 tablespoons chopped parsley

1 tablespoon chopped thyme

salt and freshly ground black pepper

To serve:

fresh coriander sprigs

char-grilled bread or boiled rice

Serves 6

1

Scrub the mussels or clams and discard any that remain open.

2

Boil the corn in unsalted water for about 8 minutes and either cut into chunks or slice the kernels off the cobs.

3

Put the squid, prawns, if using, and 1 tablespoon of the oil in a bowl with the chilli flakes, salt, pepper and half the garlic. Heat a frying pan until smoking hot and sear the squid and prawns or lobster for 1 minute. Remove from the pan and set aside.

4

Heat the remaining oil in the pan, add the shallots, carrots, coriander seeds and remaining garlic and sauté until softened but not browned. Add the wine, stock, lime juice and saffron and simmer for 5 minutes. Add the mussels or clams, corn, tomatoes and okra and simmer gently for a further 5 minutes. Add the remaining seafood, parsley and thyme, then taste and adjust the seasoning. Cook for a further 2 minutes.

5

Divide the gumbo between 6 heated bowls, top with coriander and serve with grilled bread or boiled rice.

Prawn and pea aubergine laksa

Pea aubergines, sold in Thai shops, are pea-sized and grow in bunches. They have a tart taste and light crunch. A laksa is a Malay curry with noodles. It can be kept simple with just rice vermicelli noodles and fresh herbs or made more elaborate, by adding seafood, fishcakes and condiments.

125 ml peanut or corn oil

1 stalk lemongrass, trimmed and smashed

800 ml canned coconut milk

a handful of pea aubergines or fresh peas

200 g rice vermicelli noodles

juice of ½ lime

12 large cooked prawns

sea salt and freshly ground black pepper

fresh coriander, to serve

Rempah:

50 g macadamia or cashew nuts

8 small shallots, chopped

4 garlic cloves, crushed

2 small red chillies, chopped

2 cm fresh turmeric root, peeled and chopped (optional)*

3 cm fresh galangal or ginger, chopped

2 teaspoons chopped coriander root or 1 teaspoon coriander seeds

1 teaspoon shrimp paste (*blachan*) or anchovy essence

Serves 6

1

Put all the rempah ingredients in a blender or food processor and blend to a paste. Heat the oil in a saucepan or wok, add the paste and stir-fry until darkened. Strain off the excess oil.

2

Add the lemongrass, 200 ml water and the coconut milk and bring to a fast simmer. When the liquid has reduced and thickened a little, add the pea aubergines or peas and simmer gently for about 10 minutes.

3

Soak the rice noodles in a bowl of hot water until soft – about 15 minutes. Drain and divide between 6 bowls.

4

Season the soup with the lime juice, salt and pepper, then ladle over the noodles. Add plenty of fresh coriander and 2 prawns to each bowl.

Note: *Turmeric root is available from Asian markets. It doesn't have a great deal of flavour and is mainly used for its colour. The dazzling ochre-coloured juices stain everything, including fingers – so handle with care.*

Variations:

• Other cooked seafood, such as squid, octopus, fish pieces, crispy fishcakes, mussels or clams can be added.

• Cooked sliced meat or poultry, spicy meat balls or poached egg, other vegetables, crisp shallots and Asian herbs can be added.

Lemon herb-cured salmon trout with dill potatoes

Home curing is easier than you think. Sprinkle the fish with the ingredients, wrap and chill for 2 days. That's all – just remember to start 2 days before you want to eat it. The salmon trout is delicious with this potato salad but is also great served on buttered toast with a good squeeze of lemon juice.

1 salmon or salmon trout, 1.5 kg, filleted (skin-on)

3 tablespoons sea salt

3 tablespoons sugar

2 teaspoons lemon zest

2 tablespoons akvavit or vodka

1 bunch of dill, chopped

1 bunch of chives, chopped

1 bunch of flat leaf parsley, chopped

1 bunch of chervil, chopped

1 bunch of basil, chopped

young salad leaves, to serve

Dill potato salad:

2 tablespoons finely chopped red onion

2 tablespoons white wine vinegar

2 teaspoons sugar

2 tablespoons chopped fresh dill

1 tablespoon fresh lemon juice

500 g baby new potatoes, boiled and cooled

4 tablespoons sour cream

2 teaspoons freshly grated horseradish

sea salt and freshly ground black pepper

Serves 4–6

1

Put the fillets, skin side down, on a large piece of clingfilm. Remove any pin bones (they run down the lateral line). Mix the salt, sugar, lemon zest, akvavit or vodka, dill, chives, parsley, chervil and basil in a bowl, then press onto the flesh. Wrap tightly in clingfilm, put on a shallow tray and weigh down. Refrigerate for 1 day, then turn it over and refrigerate again. After 2 days, unwrap and rinse off the curing ingredients with cold running water. Pat dry with kitchen paper. Cover with more finely chopped herbs, then wrap in clingfilm until just before serving.

2

To make the potato salad, put the onion in a bowl with the wine vinegar, sugar, dill, lemon juice and salt and pepper. Marinate for 20 minutes, then add the potatoes, sour cream and horseradish. Serve in 1 large or 4 or 6 small bowls.

3

Finely slice the salmon crossways into strips, leaving the skin behind. Serve on a bed of leaves.

Pastrami salmon with caraway celeriac

The salmon is flavoured with pastrami-cure style ingredients: it semi-cures overnight. If you want to inject loads of flavour, leave the spices and herbs on for a further day or two, but even just 2–4 hours works wonders. Salmon also loves salt (it brings out the flavour and firms up the flesh) and when seared until blackened on both sides, the flavours are intensified. Freshly grated celeriac can be bought in pillow packs from specialist greengrocers.

1 kg salmon fillet (middle cut of a large salmon), skin on, pin bones removed

1 tablespoon olive oil

Pastrami cure:

1 tablespoon salt

1 tablespoon sugar

1 teaspoon ground allspice

1 teaspoon paprika

1 teaspoon garlic powder

1 teaspoon onion powder

1 tablespoon wholegrain or mild mustard

2 tablespoons finely chopped chives

2 tablespoons finely chopped dill, plus a few sprigs, to serve

Caraway celeriac:

1 celeriac (about 500 g)

juice of 1 lemon

2 tablespoons butter

1 shallot, finely chopped

1 teaspoon caraway seeds

100 ml white wine

150 ml double cream

1 teaspoon mustard powder

salt and freshly ground black pepper

1

To make the pastrami cure, mix all the ingredients in a bowl. Rub it over the flesh side of the salmon, wrap tightly in clingfilm, put in a shallow dish, weight down with a food can and chill overnight.

2

Peel the celeriac, cut into quarters and dip in a bowl of water acidulated with half of the lemon juice to prevent browning. Using a food processor or mandoline, cut the celeriac into long, fine julienne strips (a normal grater will give you a mush) and immerse in the acidulated water.

3

Drain the celeriac. Heat the butter in a small frying pan, add the shallot and sauté until soft and translucent. Add salt, pepper and caraway seeds and cook for 1 minute without browning. Add the wine and remaining lemon juice and reduce until syrupy. Stir in the cream, mustard powder and celeriac and gently cook until just softened, about 3 minutes. Taste and adjust the seasoning.

4

Scrape the pastrami cure off the salmon and rub with the oil. Heat a heavy-based frying pan until smoking hot (turn on the extraction fan) and sear the fillet, skin side down, for about 3 minutes. Don't move it – it's meant to blacken, but won't taste burnt. Slide a fish slice under the fish, turn it over and sear for 2 minutes. It should be opaque and undercooked in the middle. Slice into 6 and serve with the caraway celeriac.

Serves 6

Blackened salmon

with oven-roasted tomato salad

I like my salmon undercooked. Opaque, moist and succulent. And this is it – perfect salmon in a matter of minutes. Serve it warm or at room temperature. Oven-roasted tomatoes taste like a cross between roasted and sun-dried tomatoes: the slow drying process concentrates the tomato flavour and much improves fresh tomatoes low on flavour.

12 plum tomatoes, quartered

6 teaspoons dried oregano

750 g thick salmon fillet, skin on

2 teaspoons paprika

1 garlic clove, crushed

sea salt and freshly ground black pepper

olive oil, for brushing

Dressing:

6 tablespoons virgin olive oil

1½ teaspoons balsamic vinegar

Serves 6

1

Put the quartered tomatoes on a baking sheet lined with baking parchment. Sprinkle with half the oregano, salt and pepper, and brush with olive oil. Put into the oven on the bottom shelf of the oven and set to 100°C (200°F) Gas ½. Leave to dry for about 2–3 hours. Check them occasionally in case they dry too fast.

2

Rub the flesh side of the salmon fillet with the remaining oregano, paprika, garlic, salt and pepper, and then brush all over with olive oil.

3

Heat a heavy iron frying pan (preferably non-stick) until smoking hot. Add the salmon, flesh side down, and sear without moving it for 2 minutes. Turn it over (it should look blackened) and cook for a further 3 minutes: it should be rare in the middle. Remove the skin and flake the flesh into large chunks.

4

To serve, put the flaked salmon and the oven-roasted tomatoes on 6 plates. Mix the dressing ingredients together and sprinkle over each serving.

Variations:

• Add torn lettuce leaves, such as batavia (escarole) or cos, chopped avocado and fine beans.

• Serve with the tapenade cannellini beans (page 38).

• Use oven-roasted tomatoes with grilled vegetables and basil to make a ratatouille salad, or use them in Aubergine Mozzarella Lasagne (page 48).

80

Steamed sea bass

with mangetout and soy beans

Slice some ginger, garlic and spring onions, set the fish on its bed of mangetout (snowpeas) and black soy beans, and you're there – 10 minutes is all it takes. If you're not keen on handling (or for that matter seeing) a whole fish – with head, fins, tail and all – on your table, then ask your fishmonger to fillet it for you then put the two fillets together before cooking.

1 whole sea bass, about 1 kg, cleaned, scaled and washed

2 garlic cloves, sliced

4 cm fresh ginger, finely sliced

4 spring onions, trimmed, halved and shredded

½ tablespoon light soy sauce

4 teaspoons sesame oil

sea salt and black pepper or crushed Szechuan peppercorns

2 large handfuls of mangetout (snowpeas)

2 tablespoons whole black soy beans (drained if in brine), rinsed*

sprigs of coriander or Thai basil leaves, to serve

Serves 4

*Note: Salted black soy beans are available from Asian grocers. Drain and rinse off excess salt before using.

82

1

Season the fish inside and out with salt and pepper and tuck half the garlic and ginger into the cavity.

2

Lay the fish on baking parchment. Scatter the spring onions and the remaining ginger and garlic on top. Sprinkle with the soy sauce and half the sesame oil.

3

Fold over the paper to enclose the fish and crease the edges together. Place in a steamer or oven preheated to 200°C (400°F) Gas 6, and cook for 10 minutes.

4

Heat the remaining oil in a wok or large frying pan, add the mangetout and black beans and stir-fry for about 1 minute.

5

To serve, put the mangetout and beans on a warmed serving plate, lay the fish on top and pour over any cooking juices. Sprinkle with herbs and serve.

Bacon-wrapped monkfish

with Brussels tops and horseradish picada

Monkfish is a deep sea fish with a dense meaty flesh that's ideal for roasting. Brussels tops are the young leaves that crown sprout plants. They're sweet and very tender and don't taste at all sprout-like. If you can't find them, use spring greens or cabbage instead.

6 monkfish fillets,
about 1.2 kg in total

12 slices bacon

6 Brussels tops,
coarse stems removed

1 tablespoon balsamic vinegar

2 tablespoons olive oil,
plus extra for brushing

salt and freshly ground
black pepper

Horseradish picada:

75 ml olive oil, or to taste

50 g skinned hazelnuts*

50 g skinned almonds*

1 thick slice white bread

½ tablespoon sherry vinegar

2 tablespoons raisins,
soaked in sherry vinegar

3 tablespoons
creamed horseradish

salt and freshly ground
black pepper

Serves 6

Note: To skin nuts, soak for a few minutes in boiling water, then pop them out of their brown skins (almonds) or wrap them in a tea towel and rub them off (hazelnuts).

1

To make the picada, heat 1 tablespoon of the oil in a frying pan, add the nuts and gently fry until lightly browned. Remove, and fry the bread in the same oil. Put the nuts, bread, salt and pepper in a food processor and blend to a paste. With the motor running, slowly add olive oil in a thin stream until the paste becomes a thick sauce. Stir in vinegar to taste, then add the raisins and horseradish. Set aside.

2

Lightly sprinkle the monkfish with salt and pepper, wrap each piece in 2 bacon slices and put into a roasting tin. Brush the wrapped fish with olive oil and put the tin on top of the stove. Cook over a high heat until lightly brown all over. Transfer to a preheated oven and roast at 220°C (425°F) Gas 7 for 8–10 minutes. Remove from the oven. If the bacon has not crisped, brown under a hot grill.

3

Half fill a wok with water, then add salt and pepper. Bring to the boil then add the prepared Brussels tops and blanch for 1 minute. Drain off the water, then add the vinegar and 2 tablespoons olive oil, more salt and pepper and stir-fry for a further 1 minute.

4

Divide the wilted Brussels tops between 6 wide, shallow bowls. Slice each piece of monkfish into 4 and place on top of the wilted leaves. Serve with a spoonful of picada.

Rock salmon in beer batter
with pease pudding and mint vinaigrette

Rock salmon, also known as huss or dog fish, is a relation of the shark. It is a cartilaginous fish which means it has no bones and so is easy to eat. Pease pudding – a delicious pea purrée – is normally made with dried marrow fat peas but I make mine with fresh garden peas for a fresher flavour.

6 pieces of rock salmon or skate, about 225 g each

sea salt

sunflower or vegetable oil, for deep-frying

Beer batter:

200 g plain flour, sieved, plus extra for dusting

½ teaspoon sea salt

2 teaspoons baking powder

250 ml beer

2 egg whites

Pease pudding:

40 g unsalted butter

1 onion, chopped

1 thick slice of bacon

350 g shelled peas

Mint vinaigrette:

½ teaspoon sugar

leaves from 1 bunch mint, chopped

4 tablespoons virgin olive oil

2 tablespoons lemon juice

1 tablespoon balsamic vinegar

sea salt and freshly ground black pepper

Serves 6

1

To make the batter, mix the flour, salt, baking powder and beer in a bowl. Set aside for 30 minutes. Whisk the egg whites to soft peak stage and beat in just before using.

2

To make the pease pudding, melt the butter in a saucepan, add the onion and cook gently until softened and translucent, about 5–10 minutes. Add the bacon and peas and cover with water (do not salt). Bring to the boil, reduce the heat and simmer for 10 minutes. Discard the bacon, put the peas in a food processor, add salt and pepper to taste, then work to a purée. Set aside to keep warm.

3

To make the mint vinaigrette, whisk the sugar, mint, oil, lemon juice, vinegar, salt and pepper in a jug or bowl.

4

Fill a saucepan or wok one-third full of oil, heat to 190°C (375°F), or until a cube of bread browns in 30 seconds. Season and dust the fish with flour, dip in the batter and deep-fry in the oil until golden, about 4–5 minutes.

5

Serve with a spoonful of pease pudding and mint vinaigrette.

Salmon fish fingers

with asparagus, spring pods and mustard-mint butter

This asparagus mixture is wonderful on its own as a first course – or with fish, meat or poultry as a main course. Vary the ingredients according to whatever is fresh and exciting in the shops.

Fish fingers:

6 salmon fillets, about 180 g each

100 g couscous

1 garlic clove, crushed

grated zest of 1 lemon

1 teaspoon paprika

1 teaspoon ground cumin

1 teaspoon ground coriander

1 teaspoon ground ginger

flour, for dusting

2 eggs, lightly beaten

salt and pepper

butter and olive oil, for frying

30 asparagus tips

6 pattypan squash or courgettes, halved

300 g mixed pods, such as beans, sugarsnaps and mangetout

5 tablespoons butter

1 tablespoon wholegrain mustard

chopped fresh mint and chives, to serve

Serves 6

1

To make the fish fingers, pat the salmon dry with kitchen paper. Put the couscous in a bowl, add boiling water until just covered, then set aside for 5 minutes until doubled in size. Fluff up with a fork, leave 5 minutes more, then fluff up again. Spread out on a wide plate and let dry for 10 minutes. Mix with the garlic, lemon zest, paprika, cumin, coriander, ginger, salt and pepper. Dip the fish in flour, then in beaten egg, then in the couscous mixture – pat on extra. Chill for 2 minutes.

2

Blanch the asparagus, pattypans, courgettes and fine beans, if using, in boiling salted water for 1–2 minutes. Add the sugarsnaps or mangetout, if using, and blanch for 1 minute more.

3

Heat the butter and oil in a frying pan, add the fish and fry gently for 2 minutes on each side. Remove and drain on kitchen paper.

4

Heat the butter and mustard in a large shallow pan or wok, add the drained vegetables and toss well. Heat through for about 1 minute, then toss in the mint.

5

To serve, slice each fillet lengthways to make 2 'fingers'. Put 2 pieces of fish on each plate, and pile the mustard buttered vegetables on top. Sprinkle with chives and serve.

Smoked fishcakes

with lemon butter spinach

Smoked fish makes the best fishcakes. Other fish such as salmon often seem tasteless when mixed with mashed potato and fried. I've made champ, the Irish dish of mashed potato infused with spring onion, as the base for my cakes. The lemon butter is much easier to make than hollandaise.

300 ml milk

500 g smoked undyed haddock

2 tablespoons butter

4 spring onions, finely chopped

3 tablespoons double cream

800 g potatoes, cooked in boiling salted water

2 tablespoons chopped parsley

freshly grated nutmeg

plain flour, for dusting

1 egg, lightly beaten

4 tablespoons breadcrumbs (from day-old white bread)

vegetable oil, for frying

sea salt and freshly ground black pepper

Lemon butter spinach:

juice of 1 lemon

90 g butter, chilled and diced

baby spinach or pousse leaves, to serve

Makes 12 balls or 6 cakes

1

Heat the milk in a wide, shallow saucepan, add the haddock and poach for about 5 minutes. Remove from the milk and let cool. Flake the fish, removing any bones and skin. Discard the milk.

2

Heat the butter in a small saucepan over a gentle heat, add the spring onions and cream and sauté gently for about 1 minute to soften the spring onions. Add the mixture to the cooked potato and mash together. Add the parsley, nutmeg and seasoning. Mix in the flaked fish, taste and adjust the seasoning, then chill for 1 hour or overnight to firm the mixture.

3

Mould the fish and potato mixture into 12 small balls or 6 large cakes. Flour each cake, dip into the beaten egg and then pat with breadcrumbs. Chill until needed.

4

Heat the vegetable oil in a deep-fat fryer to the recommended level and temperature. Add the balls in batches and deep-fry for about 3 minutes. Alternatively, heat about 1 cm depth of oil and 1 tablespoon of butter in a large, preferably non-stick, frying pan. Add the fishcakes and fry all over until golden brown. Set aside to keep them warm.

5

Gently heat the lemon juice in a small saucepan and whisk in the chilled butter over a low heat to form an emulsion. Toss with the spinach or pousse leaves and serve with the fishcakes.

chicken and

other birds

Birds are creatures of pleasurable contrast. The cooked breast meat is different from the leg, and the crispy skin is something else, be it chicken or duck. It's this 'else' that I can't get enough of. Chicken has great lean meat, the breast is white and, if correctly cooked, succulent, while the legs are dark and almost creamy. And everything, when roasted, is jacketed in the most sought after (and fought over) crinkle-crisp, salty skin. One of the best ways to keep the breast meat of chicken moist is to pot-roast it. Duck on the other hand is best pricked all over, rubbed with salt and open-roasted on a rack as it has to shed a lot of fat as it cooks. You needn't worry about it drying out, the fat seems to constantly lubricate the meat as it melts. Gamebirds are best pot-roasted, with some liquid, plus wine or something fortified, and this will keep them plump and flavoursome. Years ago when I worked for Habitat, they sold a thing called a chicken brick. This was a rounded clay pot made up of two halves that neatly slotted together and entombed the bird. The brick sealed in all the juices of the bird and kept it very succulent while it roasted, plus you got the perfect skin on top and a stock-rich pool below. Pot-roasting is now fashionable once again. A good thing too, because, along with poaching and steaming, it's the best way to cook chicken. You can roast the bird breast side down first, then turn it, but once it's in the oven, it's nice to forget about it and life can be made even easier if the whole meal can come out of the same pot. Apart from convenience, you cash in on all of the bird's flavour, as the pot holds a sauna-like microcosm of chickeness that'll sop into anything that's nestling alongside.

Chicken and pea shoot salad

Pea shoots are the tender growing tips of mangetout plants, and need no cooking. They are commonly sold by Chinese grocers as *dau mui* and are used in salads and stir-fries. You'll need to perk them up in ice-cold water just before using. Other leaves can be used instead, such as watercress, pousse (baby spinach) or finely sliced uncooked mangetout (snowpeas). This quick salad recipe is very adaptable, so use whatever leaves you can find.

1 cooked chicken, preferably poached

3 tablespoons sour cream

3 handfuls pea shoots or mangetout

6 radishes, sliced

1 punnet cherry or baby plum tomatoes, halved

sea salt and freshly ground black pepper

Ginger marinade:

1 garlic clove, crushed

3 tablespoons rice vinegar

juice of 1 lemon

1½ tablespoons caster sugar

1 whole clove, very finely crushed

2 fresh kaffir lime leaves, very finely chopped (optional)

½ teaspoon chilli flakes

3 cm fresh ginger, finely grated, then the juice squeezed from the gratings, solids discarded

Serves 6

Variations:

• To make a different dressing, use 3 tablespoons pureéd tofu with ½ tablespoon tahini paste instead of sour cream.

• Instead of pea shoots, use other herbs, or a bag of mixed herb salad.

• Make extra dressing and toss into a rice and fresh coriander salad.

1

Remove all the meat from the chicken and pull it into shreds.

2

To make the ginger marinade, put all the ingredients in a large bowl and whisk well. Add the chicken and turn to coat thoroughly. Cover and chill for at least 1 hour or overnight.

3

Remove the chicken from the marinade. Beat the sour cream into the marinade juices, then add salt and pepper to taste.

4

Carefully fold the chicken with the pea shoots, radishes and tomatoes, then pile into bowls or onto serving plates. Spoon over the sour cream dressing and serve.

Mango lapsang chicken

and herb salad with honey and sesame dressing

To slice a mango in half you must cut parallel to the elliptical flat side of the stone. It's not as complicated as it sounds. The outward shape mirrors the internal stone: always cut lengthways with the mango positioned narrow end down. When you hit the stone, slice around it as you cut through. For this recipe choose firm fruit – too ripe and the flesh will disintegrate as you slice.

½ cooked chicken, cut in half

2 tablespoons rice vinegar

1 tablespoon caster sugar

1 garlic clove

1 bird's eye chilli, very finely chopped

shredded chicory, fresh rinsed beansprouts or baby spinach

4 spring onions, trimmed and shredded

2 handfuls coriander, mint and basil

1 very large firm mango, peeled, sides sliced off parallel to the stone, then cut into wafer-thin slices

2 tablespoons black (or white) sesame seeds, toasted in a dry frying pan

Smoking mixture (optional):

3 tablespoons Lapsang souchong tea leaves

3 tablespoons brown sugar

3 tablespoons uncooked rice

Honey and Sesame dressing:

5 tablespoons honey

3 tablespoons rice vinegar

120 ml peanut oil

2 teaspoons sesame oil

*Serves 4 as a light lunch,
8 as a first course*

1

To smoke the chicken, line the base of a steamer with a double thickness of foil. Spread the smoking mixture ingredients over the foil. Put the chicken in the steaming tray, assemble steamer and cover with a lid. Place over a gentle heat (until the smoke rises) and smoke for about 20 minutes. Alternatively, omit the smoking step and use plain cooked chicken.

2

Mix the rice vinegar, sugar, garlic and chilli and stir until the sugar has dissolved.

3

Discard the chicken skin (and smoking ingredients), flake the smoked meat from the bone and toss with the rice vinegar mixture.

4

To make the dressing, put the honey and vinegar in a food processor and blend. Gradually add the peanut and sesame oils through the feed tube of the processor, until fully amalgamated, as if making mayonnaise. The dressing should be of sauce consistency. Use half for this salad and use the remainder for other dishes.

5

Mix the chicken with the chicory, beansprouts or spinach, then add the spring onions, coriander, mint and basil. Put neat piles onto plates or into bowls, then served topped with sliced mango, the honey and sesame dressing and the toasted sesame seeds.

Grilled chicken

and pumpkin couscous with honey, mint and cardamom lemon oil

Don't be put off by the long list of ingredients – though there are many different spices, they are all quite ordinary things by today's standards and you probably have them in your cupboard already.

150 ml olive oil

20 cardamom pods, crushed

1 large whole lemon, coarsely chopped

6 chicken breast fillets

1 butternut squash, halved, deseeded and thickly sliced

1 chicken stock cube

400 g couscous

torn leaves from 1 bunch of mint, plus extra to serve

a bunch of chives, finely chopped

2 red onions, halved and finely sliced

2 garlic cloves, crushed

1 teaspoon ground cumin

1 teaspoon ground coriander

½ teaspoon ground cinnamon

a pinch of saffron (optional)

2 teaspoons clear honey

1 tablespoon pine nuts

sea salt and freshly ground black pepper

Serves 6

1

Put the oil, cardamom pods and lemon in a small frying pan and heat gently (do not fry) until the lemon peel is lightly stewed and softened. Let cool.

2

Season the chicken and squash and rub with some of the cardamom lemon oil. Preheat a stove-top grill pan (ridged, if you want black lines), add the chicken and squash and cook for 2–3 minutes on each side.

3

Dissolve the stock cube in 1 litre boiling water. Put the couscous in a bowl and pour over enough stock to barely cover (don't be tempted to add more stock). Season and leave to swell. Fluff through with a fork after 5 minutes. Stir in the mint and chives.

4

Heat 1 tablespoon of the oil in a large shallow saucepan, add the onions, garlic and ground spices and fry until the onions are soft. Add the saffron, if using, honey, pine nuts and remaining stock. Season lightly. Add the pumpkin, put the chicken on top, and heat to simmering. Partly cover the pan with a lid, then cook for about 10 minutes until the squash is just soft.

5

Divide the couscous between 6 bowls, add the spiced onion, chicken (sliced if you wish) and squash, pour over the hot juices, then serve topped with a few extra mint leaves.

Variations:

• Use cardamom lemon oil to brush meat or vegetables before grilling or roasting.

Parma chicken kiev

with peas, broad beans, mint and basil

Chicken kiev needs no introduction. We all love it. This one is made with chicken legs, which have far more succulence and flavour than breasts. It's also wrapped in Parma ham instead of breadcrumbs and roasted rather than fried. To save time, you can prepare the chicken the day before.

280 g soft butter

5 garlic cloves, crushed

5 tablespoons finely chopped parsley

2 tablespoons finely chopped basil

6 free-range chicken legs, skinned, foot joint removed, then boned*

12 thin slices Parma ham

300 g shelled fresh green peas

300 g shelled fresh broad beans

300 g yellow wax beans or green beans

a handful of fresh mint leaves

a handful of fresh basil leaves

a bunch of fresh chives

sea salt and freshly ground black pepper

olive oil, for brushing

Serves 6

Note: To bone the legs, start from the 'hip', separating the meat from the bone with the tip of a sharp knife. Follow the bone, keeping the flesh intact until you reach the 'knee'. Roll back the flesh and carefully scrape the meat from around the cartilage – don't worry about making a few holes. Proceed half way down the next bone, fold back the meat and cut off the bone. A small 'handle' of bone will remain. (Your butcher may do this job for you.)

1

Mash the butter with the garlic, parsley, basil, salt and pepper. Stuff into the leg cavities and cover the openings with the loose flap of flesh. Wrap 2 overlapping slices of Parma ham around each leg and stand them upright on in oiled roasting tin. (It can be prepared to this point, wrapped in clingfilm, refrigerated overnight, then cooked the next day.)

2

Brush the chicken with oil and roast in a preheated oven at 220°C (425°F) Gas 7 for 25 minutes or until crisp. Pierce with the point of a sharp knife: the juices will run clear when the chicken is done.

3

Simmer the peas and beans in boiling salted water until *al dente*, about 4 minutes. Drain and mix in the herbs.

4

To serve, put one Parma chicken kiev in each bowl or plate, surround with the peas, beans and leaves of mint, basil and chives. Pour over the buttery caramelized juices from the roasting tin, then serve.

Persian chicken with coconut and almonds

Almonds and pistachios, typical in Persian and Moghul cooking, are prized for their colour and flavour. The easiest way to get inside a coconut is to put it inside two plastic bags then slam it on a solid floor. Peel the skin then grate the flesh. The curry improves with time, so try to make it the day before.

6 free-range chicken legs, skinned and cut into thigh and drumstick portions

½ teaspoon ground cinnamon

½ teaspoon ground cloves

6 tablespoons sunflower oil

8 garlic cloves, chopped

5 cm fresh ginger, chopped

5 tablespoons blanched whole almonds

2 large onions, chopped

5 dried chillies

8 black cardamom pods, bruised

6 teaspoons garam masala

8 tablespoons creamy Greek yoghurt

400 ml canned coconut milk

2 tablespoons sultanas

salt

To serve:

finely grated flesh of ½ fresh coconut

2 tablespoons slivered nuts, such as almonds and pistachios

6 small bananas, such as apple bananas, peeled and sliced (optional)

Serves 6

Note: *The whole chillies and cardamoms are for flavouring only – tell your guests not to eat them.*

1

Rub the chicken pieces with the cinnamon, cloves and a little salt. Heat the oil in a non-stick frying pan, add the chicken and fry on all sides until golden. Transfer to a flameproof casserole. Retain the oil in the pan.

2

Put the garlic, ginger, almonds and onions in a food processor and work to a paste, adding a drop of water if necessary.

3

Add the chillies and black cardamom pods to the oil and fry until the chillies blister. Add the onion mixture and garam masala and fry until the paste darkens – keep stirring to avoid burning. Strain off excess oil.

4

Slowly stir in the yoghurt, 1 tablespoon at a time, then stir in the coconut milk, 100 ml water and the sultanas. Pour around the chicken in the casserole and heat to simmering. Cook, covered, in a preheated oven at 160°C (300°F) Gas 2 for 1 hour.

5

Serve topped with grated coconut, slivered nuts and banana, if using.

Clay pot lemon poussin

Lemon chicken with buttery garlic rice is my idea of perfect chicken – and putting everything in one pot is perfection too: no juices are lost and you can scrape the cooking dish clean at the table, down to every last caramelized buttery morsel. Using individual pots also makes serving easy as there's no 'dishing up' – everything is already portioned. If you haven't got four small pots, you can cook all the birds and the rice in one large pot, then serve on plates. Clay pots are available from Oriental supermarkets.

150 g butter, softened

6 garlic cloves, 4 smashed and 2 crushed

a bunch of parsley, finely chopped

4 unwaxed lemons, juice of 1, the rest cut into wedges

4 poussin (baby chickens or coquelets), preferably free-range

2 tablespoons olive oil

240 ml long-grain rice*

sea salt and freshly ground black pepper

Serves 4

Note: Measure your rice and your water in the same measuring jug.

1

Mix 120 g of the butter with the 2 crushed garlic cloves and chopped parsley. Season well.

2

Put 1 wedge of lemon, 1 smashed garlic clove and 1 heaped teaspoon of the butter mixture inside each chicken and tie the legs together with string. Rub with salt and pepper.

3

Heat the remaining butter with the oil in a large frying pan and brown the birds on all sides. Put the birds in the pots.

4

Mix the remaining garlic parsley butter with the rice and distribute around each chicken. Drizzle the lemon juice over each bird and tuck in the remaining lemon wedges. Add 100 ml water to each pot or enough water to cover the rice by 2 cm, then cover and cook in a preheated oven at 220°C (425°F) Gas 7 for 45—50 minutes. If you want greenery, serve a bowl of green beans for everyone to help themselves.

Variations:

• To make Moroccan lemon chicken, instead of parsley, mix saffron with the butter, add sultanas and toasted pine nuts to the rice and bake with preserved lemons instead of fresh. You could also rub the chicken before frying with a little paprika, ground cumin, cinnamon and ginger.

Chicken and mushroom pie

This classic pie is made extra-good with morels, which give it an added wood-smoked flavour. Dried morels are always available, and picked and dried in their prime, can be much better than many so-called 'fresh' ones.

750 g fresh, ready-made shortcrust pastry

135 g butter, softened

1 whole cooked chicken, about 2.25 kg

1 onion, quartered

2 garlic cloves

1 fresh bouquet garni of bay leaves, parsley and leek

3 blades mace or a pinch of powdered mace

750 ml good chicken stock

18 fresh morels, brushed clean, or 60 g dried (soaked in water until soft) or a mixture of wild mushrooms, including morels

1½ tablespoons plain flour

90 ml double cream

1 egg, lightly beaten

salt and freshly ground black pepper

1 fresh chanterelle, to serve (optional)

Serves 6

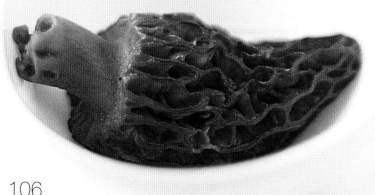

1

Roll out the pastry to 5 mm thick. Spread 45 g butter over half of the pastry and fold the other half over the top. Repeat and fold twice more. Press together and chill for 30 minutes (this will make the pastry flaky).

2

Flake the chicken into chunks. Discard the skin and bones.

3

Put the onion, garlic, bouquet garni, mace and stock in a saucepan, bring to the boil, then simmer for 10 minutes. Boil until reduced by three-quarters. Strain and discard the solids.

4

Heat the remaining butter in a frying pan, add the morels and fry for 1–2 minutes and remove. Add the flour and cook to a paste. Stir in the reduced stock and simmer to a thick sauce. Add the cream and the fried mushrooms and let boil for about 2 minutes. Taste and adjust the seasoning.

5

Roll out half the pastry and use to line a 25 cm greased pie tin or flan ring. Roll out the remaining pastry and slice into ribbons about 5 cm wide. Weave together. Fill the pastry case with the chicken and mushrooms. Pour in the cream sauce. Brush the top edge of the case with beaten egg and arrange the pastry weave on top. Trim the edges and then press together. Brush with beaten egg and bake in a preheated oven at 180°C (350°F) Gas 4 for 1 hour. Serve, topped with the fresh chanterelle, if using.

Honeyed duck

with baby chard, coriander and mustard seed mayo in ciabatta

Duck breast lends itself to fast cooking – a few minutes in a searingly hot pan is all it needs. It's at its best when the skin is caramelized to a sticky crisp, yet the meat remains rare, pink and very tender. In fact, cook the breasts as you would do for a steak. These great-tasting duck and salad pocket sandwiches could also be served in pitta bread or between toast, or just as a salad dressed with mustard seed mayo for a light lunch.

1 large Barbary duck breast

1 teaspoon five-spice powder

1 tablespoon honey

1 tablespoon light soy sauce

1 teaspoon cumin seeds

2 teaspoons sesame seeds, toasted in a dry frying pan

½ tablespoon wholegrain mustard

2 tablespoons mayonnaise

a handful of baby chard leaves or other robust salad leaves

a handful of mizuna or frisée leaves

a handful of coriander stems, coarsely chopped

a handful of spring onions, sliced lengthways into strips

ciabatta rolls, halved and hollowed, pitta breads or buttered toast

sea salt and freshly ground black pepper

Serves 4–6

1

Score fine cuts across the skin of the duck and rub with salt and five-spice powder. Pour over the honey and soy sauce, rub in, and marinate for 1–2 hours in the refrigerator.

2

Put the duck breast, skin side down, in a preheated heavy-based frying pan, and char-grill for 4 minutes. Turn it over and cook for a further 4–5 minutes. The skin will look charred but won't taste burnt: the flesh should be pink. Let it rest for 10 minutes, then cut crossways into thin slices.

3

Mix the cumin seeds, sesame seeds and mustard with the mayonnaise. Coat the inside of the breads with the mixture and stuff with remaining ingredients.

Kumquat duck with chilli citrus sauce

Kumquats or cumquats are sharply tangy and look like cocktail oranges (if there could be such a thing). It's the skin that has the flavour, don't even think of trying to peel one (you'll end up with nothing) – they're the mangetout of the citrus world and are best cooked. If you roast whole ducks, the leg meat can be shredded and used to make spring rolls and any remaining citrus sauce can be used as a dipping sauce.

3 large duck breasts

1 tablespoon honey

4 tablespoons soy sauce

salt

Chilli citrus sauce:

12 kumquats, quartered

3 cm fresh ginger, peeled and grated

2 shallots, finely sliced lengthways

2 garlic cloves, chopped

4 tablespoons sugar

1 tablespoon fish sauce

2 tablespoons rice vinegar

juice of 4 oranges, preferably blood oranges

juice of 2 limes

2 small red mild chillies, quartered and deseeded

1 tablespoon cornflour, blended with 2 tablespoons water

To serve:

2 long red mild chillies, deseeded and sliced into fine long shreds

watercress (optional)

spring onions (optional)

Serves 6

1

Using a sharp knife, finely score the duck skin. Mix the honey with the soy sauce. Rub the breasts with a little salt, then with the soy mixture, cover and chill for at least 30 minutes or overnight.

2

To make the sauce, put the kumquats, ginger, shallots, garlic, sugar and 200 ml water in a saucepan and fast simmer for about 10 minutes until reduced by half. Stir in the other ingredients, except the cornflour paste, simmer gently for 5 minutes, then strain the syrup into a clean pan. Return the kumquat peel to the syrup (discard the remaining contents of the strainer). Add the blended cornflour and boil the syrup for 1 minute to thicken.

3

Roast the duck breasts in a preheated oven at 220°C (425°F) Gas 7 for 15 minutes or until golden. Let rest for 5 minutes, then slice thickly. Reheat the sauce. Cut the duck in slices and pile in bowls, coat with the sauce, add the sliced chillies, watercress and spring onions, if using, and serve with plain boiled rice.

Variations:

• Serve the sauce with crispy reef fish: score the fish on both flanks with parallel cuts and rub with seasoning. Heat vegetable oil in a deep saucepan and slide in the fish – head first. Fry for 5–8 minutes, then serve dressed with the chilli citrus sauce and sliced shallots.

• Use the duck to make spring rolls, adding cucumber, spring onions, sesame oil, soy sauce and beansprouts. Roll up in spring roll wrappers and deep-fry in corn oil. Serve with the sauce.

Root and honey duck hot pot

For this dish, I make my own duck stock out of the pre-roasted duck carcass, but you can use four duck pieces and bought chicken stock instead. Add potatoes and squash if you want a more substantial meal, or just serve with crusty bread. Double-roasting the duck releases more fat and tenderizes the flesh, a bit like duck confit – roast it just once if you prefer it pink.

1 duck or 6 duck legs

½ teaspoon ground mace or ¼ teaspoon freshly grated nutmeg

1½ tablespoons honey

2 tablespoons olive oil

1 leek, white and pale green part only, chopped

2 stalks of green leafy celery, stalks chopped and leaves reserved

2 garlic cloves, finely chopped

1 teaspoon coriander seeds

½ teaspoon cumin seeds, toasted in a hot dry frying pan

1 litre well-seasoned chicken stock

750 g mixed root vegetables, such as parsnips or Hamburg parsley root, small turnips and salsify, all peeled and with any large roots thickly sliced

a good squeeze of fresh lemon juice

sea salt and freshly ground black pepper

Serves 6

1

If using a whole duck, prick it all over with a sharp knife (especially the flanks and fatty parts), rub with salt, pepper and mace or nutmeg. Place on a rack over a roasting tin, then rub with one tablespoon of the honey. Roast in a preheated oven at 190°C (375°F) Gas 5 for 1 hour.

2

Loosely cover with foil, let cool, then cut into quarters. Discard the ribs and backbone or use to make a stock. At this point the duck can be refrigerated for up to 3 days if you wish: it will become wrinkled and pallid, but when re-roasted will turn mahogany brown, plump and crisp.

3

If using duck portions: slash the skin and fat with a sharp knife and prepare as above. Put in a roasting tin and cook in a preheated oven at 190°C (375°F) Gas 5 for 40 minutes. Let cool as above.

4

Heat the oil in a large frying pan, add the chopped leek, celery stalks, garlic, coriander and cumin seeds and gently sauté until the vegetables have softened but not browned. Add the stock and bring to the boil, stir in the remaining honey, then add the roots and gently simmer for 25 minutes. Add the lemon juice, then taste and adjust the seasoning.

5

Meanwhile, re-roast the duck portions for 15 minutes at 220°C (425°F) Gas 7 until crisp and brown. Chop or flake the meat and distribute between 6 Chinese-style bowls. Add the soup and vegetables and top with the celery leaves.

Christmas turkey for two

with bread sauce stuffing and sprouts

You want turkey on the big day but you don't want the big bird. Easy. You can get the whole Christmas dinner experience with just a drumstick, stuffed then wrapped in bacon. Drumsticks may be considered the poor man's cut, yet the dark meat has all the flavour and the bacon wrapping keeps it moist.

150 ml milk

15 whole cloves, lightly crushed

2 bay leaves

1 onion, halved

10 thick slices white bread, crusts removed, processed to crumbs

1 turkey drumstick

6 slices unsmoked bacon,

1 tablespoon butter

about 300 g Brussels sprouts (or as many as you wish), outer leaves removed if necessary

salt and freshly ground black pepper

Serves 2

1

Put the milk, cloves, bay leaves and onion in a small saucepan, bring to the boil, then simmer gently for about 10 minutes. Let cool, then strain into another pan. Finely chop half the cooked onion and add to the milk pan. Discard the rest of the onion, the cloves and bay leaves.

2

Add the breadcrumbs to the pan, season and simmer gently, stirring, for about 5 minutes until you have a thick paste (it should be much thicker than a usual bread sauce).

3

Using a sharp narrow-bladed knife, bone the turkey drumstick, starting at the thigh end. Release the meat from the bone all the way down inside the leg. Pull out the bone. If you want a piece of bone showing (as shown in the photograph), chop off the end of the bone with a heavy cleaver and reposition it just inside the leg cavity. Stuff the leg with the bread sauce stuffing, secure the opening with cocktail sticks and rub with seasoning. Wrap the bacon in overlapping spiralling layers around the leg and put in a roasting tin. Smother with the butter and roast in a preheated oven at 200°C (400°F) Gas 6 for 50 minutes (cover with foil if the bacon starts to brown too much).

4

Cook the sprouts in boiling salted water for about 6 minutes or until tender (*al dente* is not quite cooked enough for my liking). Drain and toss in some of the turkey pan juices and serve with roast potatoes and gravy. The leg can be sliced right through into rounds – perfect portion control.

115

Pot-roasted game bird

with apple, cabbage, juniper and cream

A cross between a roast and a stew, you can put this dish in the oven, set the timer, and forget about it. This method keeps the bird moist and tender so the meat will fall from the bones, just the way you want it.

1 game bird, such as pheasant or guinea fowl, or a chicken, well seasoned

3 tablespoons olive oil

50 g butter

8 small pickling onions or shallots

2 garlic cloves, crushed

8 juniper berries, crushed

200 ml dry cider

150 ml good chicken stock

8 baby apples or 4 large, cored and quartered

greens such as the outer leaves of a Savoy cabbage, red brussels tops or black cabbage, separated into leaves, thick ribs removed

150 ml double cream

salt and freshly ground black pepper

Serves 4

1

Heat the oil and half the butter in a large frying pan, add the bird and brown it on all sides. Transfer to a deep snug-fitting flameproof casserole.

2

Wipe the pan, then add the remaining butter, onions, garlic and juniper and sauté gently for 2 minutes. Pour in the cider and stock. Simmer for 5 minutes. Add the apples and transfer to the casserole.

3

Heat to simmering, cover with a lid, then transfer to a preheated oven and cook at 180°C (350°F) Gas 4 for 45 minutes.

4

Blanch the cabbage leaves in boiling water for 3 minutes, then tuck the leaves around the bird, pour over the cream, return to the oven and cook for a further 15 minutes.

5

Cut the bird into portions and serve with the apple, cabbage and juices. Other good accompaniments are sautéed potatoes and parsnip mash flavoured with truffle oil.

Squab and peach tagine

Squab are farm-reared pigeons. Their meat is succulent and tender, far superior to wood pigeon. Consequently they're a little expensive and can be difficult to find. Duck breast, guinea fowl pieces or quail will work just as well, but remember to roast the larger birds for longer, about 20 minutes per 500 g, while the quail will only need about 8 minutes.

3 squab (French pigeon)

1 teaspoon ground ginger

½ teaspoon ground cinnamon

1 teaspoon ground mace (optional)

olive oil, for brushing and frying

4 large onions, finely sliced

4 bay leaves

a pinch of saffron (optional)

400 g couscous

chicken stock (see method)

4 garlic cloves, crushed

2 teaspoons paprika

1 teaspoon cumin

1 teaspoon coriander seeds

6 cardamom pods

1½ tablespoons pine nuts

3 tablespoons dried muscatels or large raisins

4 firm peaches, sliced into wedges

sea salt and freshly ground black pepper

Serves 6

1

Rub the squab with salt, pepper, ginger, cinnamon and mace, if using. Brush with olive oil and put on a baking sheet. Roast in a preheated oven at 200°C (400°F) Gas 6 for 15 minutes. Remove from the oven and let cool.

2

Slice the breast meat and legs from each bird and set side. Chop up the wings and carcass and put in a saucepan with 1.2 litres water. Add half a sliced onion, the bay leaves, salt and pepper. Bring to the boil, then simmer until reduced to about half volume. Strain and discard all the bones. Add the saffron to the strained stock and infuse for about 10 minutes.

3

Put the couscous in a bowl and pour in the stock until the grains are just covered. Let stand for 5 minutes, then fluff up with a fork. Keep it warm.

4

Heat 3 tablespoons olive oil in a frying pan, add the remaining onion and the garlic and sauté until soft and lightly caramelized. Add all the spices, pine nuts and muscatels or raisins and fry for a few minutes more.

5

Spoon the mixture into a shallow saucepan or frying pan with a lid. Pour over the remaining stock. Put a layer of sliced peaches on the top, followed by a layer of squab pieces. Put the lid on the pan and simmer over a low heat for about 10 minutes.

6

Serve on heated dinner plates with separate bowls of saffron couscous.

meat

There are those days when a wine-rich beef stew, a braised shoulder of lamb or joint of crackling pork is the only food that will hit the mark. It's then, when it's right miserable out, you gravitate to all things comfy, like the sofa, TV and slow-cooked food – and that means meat. In winter, little beats a pot of clove-braised cabbage with pan-crusted sausages or a melting beef suet-crust pie filled with rich onion gravy.

Spring and summer are times to enjoy faster cooked, tender cuts of lamb, rare steak or a ham, with herb olive oil or creamy buttered sauces, garden pods and leaves. Great tasting meat needs little to show it off, but make sure you buy the right cut to suit the way you're going to cook it. As a guide, the less expensive cuts of meat are marbled with fat and are suited to long slow braising, while the leaner, more expensive cuts are best cooked fast and kept rare – pork though should always be cooked right through.

And remember, the best beef, pork and lamb come from happy animals. They've been allowed to grow up as naturally as possible, to graze, root and forage in fields and fresh air, interact with each other, build muscle without in-feed antibiotics and hormones; and have been transported and slaughtered as humanely as possible. So next time you choose your joint, ask your butcher about the meat you're buying. Happy meat may cost a little more, but when you think of the life of the animal and the results, it's really worth it.

Beef stew with chestnuts

Blade of beef (from the shoulder) is the best cut of meat to use: it is marbled with fat and connective tissue and especially suited to long, slow-cooking. The meat is lubricated as it cooks, becoming moist and tender. Use fresh chestnuts or, for ease, use the peeled, part-cooked vacumn-packed variety.

1.5 kg blade or stewing steak, cut into 4 pieces*

3½ tablespoons beef dripping or olive oil

1 large onion, finely chopped

2 garlic cloves, crushed

2 bay leaves

1 star anise (optional)

2 carrots, finely chopped

2 celery stalks, finely chopped

1 tablespoon tomato purée

1½ bottles red wine

18 chestnuts

1 teaspoon sugar

salt and freshly ground black pepper

Serves 6–8

1

Rub the meat with salt and plenty of pepper. Heat a heavy, flameproof casserole until hot, add 2 tablespoons dripping or oil and add the meat. Leave without moving until well browned and caramelized, about 2 minutes. Turn over and continue browning until all sides are done. Remove from the casserole.

2

Add 1 tablespoon dripping or oil, add the onion, garlic, bay leaves, star anise, if using, carrots and celery and fry until browned. Add salt and pepper, stir in the tomato purée and cook for 1 minute. Add the wine and 300 ml water, bring to the boil, then simmer until reduced by half.

3

Put the meat back into the casserole with the vegetable wine mixture, cover, then let braise gently in a preheated oven at 150°C (300°F) Gas 2 for 3 hours.

4

If using fresh chestnuts, part-slice the chestnut skins open on their curved side, then boil for 5 minutes. Strain, cool, then peel and remove the brown pith. Heat the remaining dripping or oil in a frying pan, add the sugar and chestnuts and fry until caramelized, about 3 minutes. Add to the casserole, then return to the oven to braise for a further 40 minutes. Serve with buttery mashed potato flavoured with mustard or horseradish.

Pub beef and onion pies

The best beef and onion pies are found in British pubs. I like this easy hot water crust pastry, but you can use bought shortcrust or puff pastry instead.

45 g butter, for frying

1 kg braising steak, cubed

5 onions, 1 sliced lengthways, 4 halved and finely sliced

2 dried bay leaves, ground or very finely crumbled

2 tablespoons plain flour

2 teaspoons Worcestershire sauce

2 teaspoons tomato purée

1 teaspoon anchovy essence

1 tablespoon mushroom ketchup (sauce)

450 ml Guinness

2 teaspoons sugar

1 tablespoon wine vinegar

salt and freshly cracked black pepper

hot English mustard, to serve (optional)

Hot water crust pastry:

450 g plain flour

a large pinch of salt

170 g lard

150 ml milk

1 egg yolk, to glaze

Serves 6

6 small rectangular pie dishes

1

Heat 1 tablespoon of the butter in a deep frying pan. Season the meat and brown in batches. Remove and keep warm.

2

Heat the remaining butter in the pan, add the finely sliced onions and bay leaves and fry until lightly browned. Season, stir in the flour, adding extra butter if necessary, and fry until the onion mixture is a rich brown.

3

Stir in the Worcestershire sauce, tomato purée, anchovy essence, mushroom ketchup, Guinness, sugar and vinegar and let bubble for 5 minutes. Stir in 300 ml water, cover and simmer gently for 1½ hours. Spoon into the pie dishes.

4

To make the pastry, sift the flour and salt into a bowl. Put the lard, milk and 150 ml water in a saucepan and bring to the boil. Stir into the flour, let cool, then knead gently but firmly. Use immediately – do not refrigerate.

5

Roll out the pastry to 5 mm thick. Cut 6 rectangles to fit the tops of the pie dishes and press an onion slice into each. Cut small strips from the remaining pastry and use to line the rim of each dish, pressing firmly. Place a pastry lid on top and, using your fingers or tip of a knife, press the edges onto the pastry-lined rim to seal. Make a small hole in the top of each pie to let the steam escape, brush with egg yolk and bake in a preheated oven at 200°C (400°F) Gas 6 for 30 minutes.

6

Serve with mustard, if using, and boiled potatoes or mash.

Lamb burgers
with char-grilled aubergine, hoummus, seed salt and mint

Homemade burgers are vastly superior to shop-bought ones, and so easy to make that we should all make them more often – everyone loves a burger. The seed salt is delicious – store the extra and use it in lots of other ways.

2 tablespoons olive oil

1 onion, finely chopped

2 cloves garlic, crushed

1 small chilli, very finely chopped (optional)

500 g lamb mince

a handful of mint leaves, chopped, plus extra leaves to serve

1 aubergine, sliced lengthways

sea salt and freshly ground black pepper

150 g hoummus, to serve

Seed salt:

1 tablespoon cumin seeds

1 tablespoon sesame seeds

1 tablespoon sea salt

Makes 6 burgers

1
To make the seed salt, toast the cumin seeds and sesame seeds in a dry frying pan until the sesame seeds are a light golden brown (watch them, and turn them regularly – they'll burn if left alone). Mix in a bowl with the salt.

2
Heat half the olive oil in the frying pan, add the onion, garlic, chilli, 2 teaspoons seed salt and black pepper and sauté until the onion is soft and transparent.

3
Put the lamb mince in a bowl with the chopped mint, the onion mixture, salt and freshly ground black pepper. Mix well. Shape into burgers, brush with oil and cook under a hot grill or in a preheated stove-top grill pan until crisp and brown outside and pink in the middle. Remove and drain on kitchen paper.

4
Brush the aubergine slices on both sides with the remaining oil and season with salt and pepper. Char-grill on both sides until seared with black lines and softened.

5
Serve the lamb burgers topped with a spoonful of hoummus and a fold of aubergine, sprinkled with a little seed salt and a few mint leaves.

Variations:

• To make *baba ganoush*, mash the aubergine with lemon juice, tahini, olive oil, crushed garlic, seed salt and chopped mint – serve with minted lamb meat balls (use burger mixture).

127

Rosemary and olive lamb

with roasted garlic butter beans

I've used rack of lamb but if you are cooking for more than four people you should use leg or shoulder as in the variation. If you've just decided you want to cook this today, use canned butter beans instead (omit step 1) – cannellini or flageolet beans are equally good.

650 g dried butter beans, soaked overnight in cold water to cover, then drained

1 onion

2 whole heads of garlic, separated into cloves (skin on)

½ lamb or chicken stock cube, crumbled

1 fresh bouquet garni (fresh bay leaves, sprigs of thyme, parsley and rosemary)

1 rack of lamb (total 12 ribs), trimmed of excess fat

leaves from 1 small bunch of rosemary, chopped

8 black olives, pitted and chopped

2 tablespoons olive oil

sea salt and freshly ground black pepper

Serves 4–6

1

Put the beans, onion, 4 peeled garlic cloves, stock cube and bouquet garni in a saucepan, cover with cold water and bring to the boil. Skim off any foam, lower the heat after 5 minutes and gently simmer for 1 hour or until the beans are tender (season only during the last 10 minutes of cooking). Let cool in the juices. Discard the onion, garlic and bouquet garni.

2

Rub the lamb with salt and pepper and coat the fat side with the chopped rosemary and chopped olives, pressing on well. Put the rack of lamb in a roasting tin, tuck the unpeeled garlic cloves underneath and spoon the oil over the top. Roast in a preheated oven at 200°C (400°F) Gas 6 for 20–25 minutes until the meat is medium-rare or until cooked to your liking.

3

Meanwhile, reheat the beans in their stock. When the lamb is cooked, remove from the tin, cover with foil and let rest for 5 minutes. Pop the garlic cloves out of their papery skins, strain the beans and mix with the roasted garlic cloves in the roasting tin. Transfer to a warmed serving dish. Slice the lamb and place on top of the roasted garlic butter beans.

Variations:

• If using a leg of lamb, roast for 20–25 minutes per 500 g, adding the garlic to the roasting tin 25 minutes before the end of the cooking time. Let the meat rest for 10 minutes before carving. If you need to keep everything warm, the cooked beans and skinned garlic cloves can be spooned around the lamb in the tin.

• If using shoulder of lamb, open-roast until brown, then put in a casserole and braise with the beans until meltingly tender.

Lamb shanks
with autumn squash ratatouille

Lamb shank is the upper foreleg of the animal. Allow for 3 hours of slow braising – this one can't be rushed. In fact the shanks taste better if cooked the day before (until stage 3) and left to saturate and cool in their juices; the final result is meat that is meltingly tender and falls from the bone.

6 lamb shanks, trimmed

5 garlic cloves, cut into slivers

4 tablespoons olive oil, for frying, plus extra, for brushing

2 onions, finely chopped

2 carrots, finely chopped

3 sticks celery, finely chopped

2 tablespoons tomato paste

3 bay leaves

3 strips orange peel

300 ml white wine

3 red peppers, deseeded and sliced, or 3 Italian sun-dried red peppers*

1 butternut or acorn squash, halved lengthways, peeled, deseeded and sliced

1 tablespoon capers

150 g black olives, pitted if preferred

small bunch basil, leaves only

sea salt and freshly ground black pepper

Serves 6

From Italian delicatessens.

1
Season the lamb and stab all over with a knife. Insert the garlic slivers into the incisions. Heat 2 tablespoons of the oil in a large, heavy-based frying pan. Brush each shank with olive oil, add to the pan in batches and fry until brown on all sides. Remove and set aside. Add a little more oil to the pan and heat gently.

2
Add the onion, carrot and celery and fry until browned. Mix in the tomato paste, bay leaves, orange peel and seasoning. Cook for 2 minutes. Add the wine and 300 ml water, bring to the boil then simmer until reduced by half. Transfer to a small, deep roasting tin.

3
Add the lamb shanks, cover tightly with foil and cook in a preheated oven at 150°C (300°F) Gas 3 for 2 hours.

4
Heat the remaining oil in the frying pan. Brush the peppers with olive oil and season with salt and freshly ground black pepper. Add to the pan and cook until lightly browned on both sides. Add to the lamb shanks, then add the squash, capers, olives and a little extra water if necessary. Continue braising for 1 hour or until the squash is tender.

5
Remove from the oven, then top with the basil leaves and serve with creamy mashed potato or crusty bread.

Pork chops with peppered wild mushroom gravy

No-nonsense pork chops with a rich autumnal mushroom gravy and a bowl of mash to mop it up – heart-warming stuff. Any mixture of wild funghi will do, including chanterelles and porcini, but you can also achieve good results with large open-cap mushrooms or smaller brown-capped chestnuts (slip in few slices of dried porcini to get the 'wild' flavour).

60 g butter

3 tablespoons olive oil

4 garlic cloves, finely chopped

2 onions, chopped

3 bay leaves

4 tablespoons sherry vinegar

220 ml sherry or Madeira

20 g dried porcini, soaked in 150 ml hot water until soft

800 ml chicken stock

6 pork chops or loin steaks, trimmed of excess fat

450 g mixed wild and cultivated mushrooms

sea salt and freshly ground black pepper

creamy mashed potato, to serve (optional)

Serves 6

1

Heat half the butter and half the olive oil in a frying pan, add half the garlic, the onion, bay leaves and seasoning and sauté until the onion becomes transparent. Add the sherry vinegar and reduce until almost dry, then add the sherry, the porcini, their soaking water and the stock to the pan and simmer for 20 minutes or until reduced by half. Strain into a clean, wide saucepan and discard all the residue, including the porcini.

2

Heat a ridged stove-top grill pan or heavy-based frying pan until smoking hot. Rub the pork with salt, pepper and a little of the olive oil and char-grill for 4 minutes on each side.

3

Cut medium-sized mushrooms in half, trim off any woody stem tips and slice any large cap mushrooms. Heat the remaining oil and butter in the frying pan, add the mushrooms and the remaining garlic and sauté about 2 minutes or until tinged golden brown. Season, then add to the pan of gravy and reheat.

4

Serve the chops, mushroom gravy and mashed potato, if using, on preheated plates and sprinkle generously with pepper.

Anise braised pork

with Chinese mustard cabbage

Pork meat has a tendency to dry out when roasted, so braising it – as they do in Peking – semi-immersed in honey-sweetened soy sauce keeps it succulent and, of course, steeps the meat with plenty of Chinese flavour. Don't worry about the quantity of soy sauce – it's for poaching, not eating, and you can freeze it to use again.

1 kg boned pork leg

2 teaspoons five-spice powder

3 tablespoons peanut oil

1 bottle Kikkoman soy sauce (400 ml)

6 small pink shallots, or 1–2 large

4 cm fresh ginger, sliced

3 garlic cloves, sliced

2 small fresh whole red chillies

4 tablespoons mirin (rice wine)

1 tablespoon golden syrup or honey

4 whole star anise

1 Chinese mustard cabbage (*dai gai choi*) or other Chinese greens

sea salt

Serves 6

1

Score the pork rind with diagonal cuts. Put in a colander and pour over a kettle of boiling water. Pat dry with kitchen paper. Rub a little salt and five-spice powder into the scored skin. Heat 2 tablespoons of the oil in a frying pan, add the pork, skin side down, and fry until lightly scorched. Add 3 tablespoons soy sauce and reduce until caramelized. Transfer the pork to a casserole or sand pot.

2

Heat the remaining oil in the pan, add the shallots, ginger, garlic and chillies and fry until browned. Add the mirin, golden syrup, star anise, remaining soy sauce and 600 ml water. Stir to dissolve the syrup. Transfer to the casserole.

3

Bring to the boil, cover, turn the heat to low and simmer gently for 2–2½ hours until meltingly tender. Put the mustard cabbage leaves around the pork and braise for 5 minutes more.

4

Slice the pork and serve with the cabbage and a few spoonfuls of the casserole juices.

Pecan pork with apple and maple syrup

Boneless loin of pork is perfect for stuffing. You'll need string and bamboo skewers to hold the stuffing in place. Remove the string before serving, but leave the skewers in the meat to hold each portion together.

1 loin of pork, about 1.5 kg, trimmed but with skin included

½ teaspoon ground allspice

3 tablespoons olive oil

5 tablespoons maple syrup

30 g butter

6 apples, cored and quartered

salt and freshly ground black pepper

Pecan stuffing:

150 g shelled pecans

1 onion, chopped

2 garlic cloves, crushed

leaves from 1 bunch of flat leaf parsley

1 bunch of sage, stems discarded

100 g fresh breadcrumbs

2 cloves, ground

1 egg, lightly beaten

salt and freshly ground black pepper

Serves 6

1

To make the stuffing, work the nuts in a food processor until finely chopped but not ground. Transfer to a large bowl. Add the onion, garlic and herbs to the processor and chop finely.

2

Heat 2 tablespoons olive oil in a frying pan, add the onion mixture and cook gently until softened. Stir into the pecan mixture, then stir in the ground cloves, salt, pepper and egg. Open up the natural cavity in the joint and stuff with the pecan stuffing. Close up and tie the length of the loin with string.

3

Place the meat in a roasting tin. Using a craft knife or very sharp kitchen knife, score the skin and fat with fine parallel slashes. Pierce and secure at regular intervals with bamboo or wooden skewers. Rub with plenty of salt, pepper, allspice and the remaining oil. Roast in a preheated oven at 220ºC (425ºF) Gas 7 for 30 minutes. Pour over half the maple syrup, lower the heat to 190ºC (375ºF) Gas 5, then roast for a further 45 minutes.

4

Heat the butter in a frying pan, add the apple quarters and fry until lightly browned. Pour in the remaining maple syrup and cook for about 2 minutes until lightly caramelized. Arrange around the pork for the last 10 minutes of cooking. Remove from the oven and set aside, loosely covered with foil, for 10 minutes before carving. To serve, slice the pork as skewered portions and serve with celeriac or parsnip mash.

Ham and peas

Many meals can be made from a single ham hock – the flakes of succulent meat and the aromatic saturated stock can be used separately or together to make robust, yet elegant, fare. This is real home cooking, but if you don't want to cook your own ham for the salad variation, use store-bought ham.

1 unsmoked ham hock, about 2 kg

2 bay leaves

stems of flat leaf parsley

1 teaspoon dried oregano

2 garlic cloves

1 onion, halved

1 teaspoon freshly grated nutmeg

1 tablespoon peppercorns

500 g shelled green peas

a handful of cooked and skinned broad beans (optional)

leaves from 1 bunch of mint, torn

sea salt

Roasting mix:

1 tablespoon olive oil

1 tablespoon clear honey

3 teaspoons sea salt

5 whole cloves, ground

freshly ground black pepper

Serves 6

1

Put the ham hock into a deep saucepan and just cover with cold water. Add salt and bring to the boil on top of the stove. Skim off the foam, then add the bay leaves, parsley, oregano, garlic, onion, nutmeg and peppercorns. Cover and simmer gently for 1 hour.

2

Lift the ham from the saucepan and strain the stock. Slash the skin and rub with olive oil, salt, honey, ground cloves and black pepper. Put in a roasting tin and cook in a preheated oven at 220°C (425°F) Gas 7 for 45 minutes. If it browns too quickly turn the heat down to 200°C (400°F) Gas 6.

3

Put the peas and broad beans, if using, in the roasting tin, fill 1 cm deep with ham stock, and cook for about 5 minutes. Remove from the oven.

4

Slice the ham and serve hot, with the peas, beans and mint leaves.

Variation:

• This recipe is also good served cold as a pea and ham salad with a parsley and mustard dressing. Whisk 2 teaspoons Dijon mustard in a bowl with 2 tablespoons cider vinegar and 3 tablespoons olive oil. Beat in a pinch of sugar, a handful of chopped parsley, some chopped green peppercorns and 1 crushed garlic clove.
To serve, toss the peas with a chopped shallot, torn mint leaves and olive oil. Add sliced ham and pour over the dressing.

Allspice cabbage
with shallots and sausages

You can use any type of sausage for this recipe: Cumberland, herb, game, Toulouse or Cajun – the choice is yours. Braised red cabbage is so versatile, it can be left for ages in the oven: it will wait for you rather than you for it. No wonder it's a classic. If everyone is late for supper, just put the cooked sausages in the casserole with the cabbage and keep everything on a low heat until you're ready to eat.

1 red cabbage, halved, cored and cut into chunks (leaves separated)

4 large banana shallots or 8 shallots, peeled

1 garlic clove, crushed

½ teaspoon crushed cloves

½ teaspoon ground cinnamon

½ teaspoon ground allspice

½ teaspoon freshly grated nutmeg

1½ tablespoons brown sugar

2 tablespoons apple or cranberry jelly

3 tablespoons red wine vinegar

30 g butter, softened

salt and freshly ground black pepper

12 sausages of your choice, such as regular, herb, game or Toulouse

Serves 6

1
Put all the ingredients except the sausages in a heavy casserole, add 3 tablespoons water and mix well.

2
Cover with a lid and braise in a preheated oven at 150°C (300°F) Gas 2 for 2 hours. Stir twice during the cooking time so the cabbage and shallots receive their fair share of spice and buttery juices.

3
Grill or fry the sausages until cooked and well browned all over. If the cabbage is not quite ready, put the sausages on top of the cabbage in the casserole to keep hot. If using banana shallots, remove them from the casserole and cut in half lengthways before serving. Serve with a generous helping of mustard mash.

Variations:

• Add sultanas or prunes, chopped chilli and paprika and serve with roast honeyed duck (page 108) or duck confit.

• Add sliced apples and serve with roast pork or grilled goats' cheese.

As far as I'm concerned a pudding can be eaten at any time of the day. A tart or pastry for breakfast or with a mid-morning coffee can be just the thing you crave to whip up some energy; ice cream on a sweltering afternoon cools, soothes and relaxes; and a slice of cake or chocolate shortbread with your afternoon cuppa is just the boost you need at the end of the day. Then there's dinner time pudding, and for some – girlies mainly – it's the best bit of the meal. That makes at least four puddings you can fit, if somewhat tightly, into your day.

When you've got your mates round for dinner, the last place you should be is in the kitchen. Pudding should have been sorted out well before they descend. They're not there to get all impressed at how clever you are – well, just a little maybe. Anyhow, from my experience if you leave the table for too long, they'll come and find you in the kitchen and start chatting and distracting you from anything you might have planned to be doing. So make sure you've made the pudding well in advance and preferably something that can be served cold or only needs a few minutes in the oven. Something that is simple will look chic because it is so simple. For instance, I think pears are best kept whole or almost whole – you can never chop up a pear, rearrange it and make it look better. Somehow you've just lost its perfect shape. This is why poached pears look so perfect and why I've used them simply halved with stems still attached in my pear tart recipe. The same applies to berries, figs, peaches and many others. This simplicity is important in all puddings, even those that use the fruit as a flavouring, a filling or a sauce. If the ingredients are good then you don't need to create elaborate puddings. What a stroke of luck – it makes pudding courses so easy.

puddings

Raspberry ripple

Shop-bought ripple is not what it used to be. This one is the real thing and looks the part, with pure vanilla ice cream, streaked with painterly lines of fresh raspberry purée. A classic combination.

600 ml milk

1 vanilla pod, split lengthways

250 g caster sugar

7 egg yolks

600 ml double cream, whipped to soft peak stage

Ripple:

220 g raspberries, plus extra to serve

60 g caster sugar

1 tablespoon lemon juice

1
Put the milk and vanilla pod in a saucepan. Bring to the boil, remove from the heat and let cool for 30 minutes. Discard the vanilla pod.

2
Beat the sugar and egg yolks in a bowl, then pour in the vanilla milk. Put into a saucepan and heat gently, stirring continuously, until you have a thin custard (too much heat and the custard will curdle and separate). Cool, then chill. Fold the whipped cream into the cold custard, pour into a covered container, then freeze.

3
Put the raspberries, sugar, lemon juice and 1 tablespoon water into a saucepan, bring to the boil, reduce the heat and simmer until soft. Push the mixture through a non-metal sieve into a bowl. Chill.

4
Remove the ice-cream from the freezer and let soften until spreadable. Spoon one-third of the mixture into a shallow square or rectangular container lined with clingfilm. Mark parallel uneven furrows in the ice cream, then pipe the raspberry purée into the furrows. Carefully spread over another layer of softened ice-cream, repeating until all the ice-cream and raspberry mixture has been used. Finish with more wobbly stripes of ripple. Freeze until set.

5
To serve, remove from the container, discard the clingfilm and trim the sides straight if necessary. Serve alone or with fresh raspberries.

Serves 4–6

Rosewater-poached rhubarb
with vanilla ricotta

Rhubarb needs the briefest of cooking – especially if you want the stems to keep their shape. Forced rhubarb, around in spring, has the best pink colour.

450 g rhubarb, cut into bite-sized chunks

150 g sugar

a squeeze of lemon juice

1½ tablespoons rosewater

600 g buffalo ricotta cheese

1 vanilla pod, split lengthways

1 tablespoon caster sugar

3 tablespoons double cream

Serves 6

Variations:

• Serve the rhubarb with mascarpone beaten with ground almonds and vanilla sugar.

• Add a pinch of saffron threads or slivers of candied ginger to the rhubarb juice.

• Serve the vanilla ricotta with a pile of berries or bake into a cheesecake and top with the poached rhubarb.

1

To cook the rhubarb, put the sugar, lemon juice and 125 ml water into a saucepan, stir and bring to the boil. Turn down the heat and simmer gently until all the sugar has dissolved. Add the chunks of rhubarb and stir again to coat. Simmer for about 3 minutes. Gently turn over the rhubarb, cover the pan with a lid, turn off the heat, stir in the rosewater and let cool.

2

Using a wooden spoon, press the ricotta through a sieve into a bowl. Scrape the seeds from the vanilla pod into the ricotta and mix well. Dissolve the sugar in the cream and beat into the ricotta. Chill.

3

Spoon the rhubarb and rosewater juices into bowls or onto small serving plates and serve with the vanilla ricotta in spoonfuls, or in a separate bowl.

Caramel syrup apples

with thick whipped cream

I love tarte Tatin – the soaked flaky pastry is good, but what makes it for me is the combination of melting apple saturated in caramel and all that extra buttery syrup that runs in rivulets into a pool of cream on the plate. So why not do just that. Forget about pastry, and have apples, buttery caramel and loads of cream. A seriously sensuous windfall in a bowl.

6 medium apples

juice of 1 lemon

500 g caster sugar

100 g butter

1 teaspoon ground cinnamon

300 ml double cream, whipped, or crème fraîche

Serves 6

1

Peel the apples and put into a bowl of water mixed with lemon juice to stop them turning brown.

2

Put the sugar into a small saucepan with 1 tablespoon water, and cook over a gentle heat until golden and turned to a light caramel. Stir in the butter.

3

Drain the apples, pack into a deep dish, sprinkle with cinnamon and pour over the toffee caramel. Cover loosely with foil and bake in a preheated oven at 180°C (350°F) Gas 4 for 45 minutes or until the apples are very tender.

4

Serve in bowls with whipped cream or crème fraîche.

Blistered peaches with chilli kaffir lime ice

Chilli and kaffir lime ice is addictive. It may sound strange but it works. The sharp iciness of the lime kicks in first and the chilli infusion adds a warming aftertaste. Particularly good with these muscovado caramelized peaches.

3 large peaches, halved and pitted

2 tablespoons dark muscovado sugar

1 teaspoon ground allspice

30 g butter, softened

Kaffir lime ice:

5 limes, preferably kaffir limes
(grated zest of 2, juice of 5)

3 small hot chillies, split and deseeded

190 g icing sugar, sieved

450 ml crème fraîche

3 tablespoons iced water

Serves 6

1

To make the ice, put the lime zest and juice, the chillies and icing sugar in a bowl and mix to dissolve the sugar. Set aside for 30 minutes to develop the flavours.

2

Remove and discard the chillies. Beat the crème fraîche thoroughly into the lime syrup. Spoon into a covered container and freeze – there is no need to stir. Remove from the freezer and leave at room temperature for 10 minutes before serving.

3

Just before serving, sprinkle the peach halves with sugar and allspice, then smear over the butter. Lightly brown under a hot grill. Put half a peach in each serving bowl and serve with spoonfuls of ice.

Variations:

• For a lighter ice, use whipped double cream instead of crème fraîche.

• Serve the ice with fried or grilled bananas, or stir through raspberry purée to make a ripple.

• Serve the peaches with crème fraîche beaten with ginger syrup or toasted pine nuts and yoghurt.

151

Ginger toffee pears with rice pudding

Rice pudding isn't just nursery food – it's rib-sticking good, as my grandfather used to say. Sometimes, a bit of plain honest home cooking is just what we need, but with these toffee pears, it's good enough for a dinner party.

6 unripe pears, peeled

1 vanilla pod, split lengthways

120 g caster sugar

juice of ½ lemon

Vanilla rice pudding:

450 ml round pudding rice, washed

1 litre milk

200 ml double cream

1 vanilla pod, split lengthways

60 g caster sugar

Ginger toffee:

4 cm fresh ginger, chopped

150 g caster sugar

40 g unsalted butter

Serves 6

1

To make the rice pudding, pour boiling water over the rice and soak for 3 minutes. Drain, put into a saucepan, add the milk, vanilla pod and sugar and simmer gently for 30 minutes. Discard the pod, stir in the cream and spoon into a gratin dish. Cook in a preheated oven at 150°C (300°F) Gas 2 for 45 minutes.

2

To prepare the pears, put all the ingredients in a saucepan and cover with water. Simmer for 25–30 minutes or until tender. If not using immediately, let cool in the syrup. When ready to serve, remove from the syrup and heat through on top of the rice pudding.

3

To make the toffee, put the ginger, sugar and 2 tablespoons water into a small saucepan and heat gently until the mixture becomes a good caramel colour (watch it, as soon as it goes a deep red-amber colour, it's close to burning). Stir in the butter, then add 5 tablespoons water and stir well. Strain to remove the pieces of ginger. Pour some of the toffee over the pears, and serve the rest in a jug.

Lemongrass yoghurt rice

with crushed raspberries

Mix and match the refreshing lemongrass yoghurt rice with the sweet crushed fruit as you go – or you could even spoon the berries and juice into the bowls first and cover with the rice, then dig deep for the berries as you eat.

250 g raspberries

120 g caster sugar

1 tablespoon lemon juice

115 g pudding rice, washed

4 stalks lemongrass, trimmed and smashed open

700 ml milk

440 g creamy yoghurt

Serves 6

1

Put half the raspberries in a saucepan and stir in half the sugar and 1 tablespoon water. Bring to the boil, then reduce the heat and simmer until the fruit is soft. Push the fruit and juice through a non-metal sieve into a bowl, discarding the pips. Stir in the lemon juice, then add the remaining raspberries to the purée, crush lightly and let cool.

2

Put the rice, lemongrass, milk and the remaining caster sugar into a saucepan, bring to the boil, stir well, reduce the heat and simmer for 30 minutes. Let cool, then discard the lemongrass.

3

Stir the yoghurt into the lemongrass rice, then divide between 6 bowls and serve with small bowls of crushed raspberries.

Variations:

• Flavour the rice with a split vanilla pod rather than lemongrass and serve with a purée of mixed berries.

• Serve the raspberries with Greek yoghurt and honey, scattered with slivers of toasted almonds.

154

Summer pudding toast

Traditional English summer pudding, made from melted berries and juice-soaked bread, is delicious, but needs planning, to give it time to saturate and set. This combination of berry juices and strawberries on toast is an instant version – though the fruit mixture will still benefit from being left for a few hours if you have time. It looks just as elegant as the original.

4 punnets mixed berries, such as redcurrants, raspberries, blueberries and blackberries (about 500 g)

125 g sugar

250 g strawberries, stems removed and halved

6 slices brioche or white bread

To serve:

wild strawberries (optional)

mint leaves

icing sugar, for dusting

thick double cream

Serves 6

1
Pick over the punnets of fruit, removing any stems or leaves. Put the berries in a saucepan with 60 ml water and the sugar. Bring to the boil, then reduce the heat and simmer gently for about 8 minutes.

2
Put the halved strawberries in a bowl and press the cooked fruit syrup through a sieve over the strawberries. Let stand for at least 30 minutes, then chill. Alternatively, leave overnight in the refrigerator.

3
When ready to serve, toast the brioche or bread and spoon the fruit syrup over each slice. Arrange the glazed strawberries over the tops, surround with wild strawberries, if using, and sugar-dusted mint leaves. Serve the cream in a separate bowl or jug.

Variations:

- You needn't sieve the fruit, just pile it all on toast, top with thick cream and serve.
- Try using warmed doughnuts instead of toast.
- Serve the berry juice and strawberry mixture with vanilla ice cream.

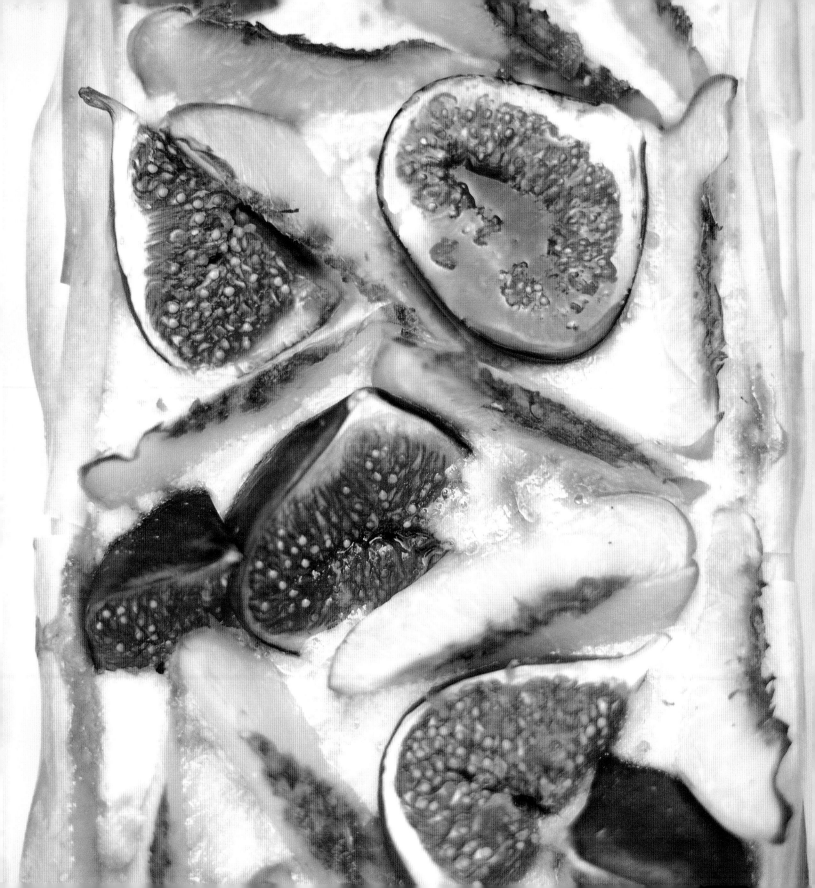

Peach and fig almond tart

A fail-safe pudding, that's very straight forward – and there's no pastry to make or roll out. The fruit just gets on with the work as it bakes, creating a wonderful soft almond and blistered fruit filling, oozing nectar-like juice.

8 sheets filo pastry, or enough to make 4 layers

melted butter, for greasing and brushing

1 tablespoon caster sugar

1 egg, lightly beaten

250 g mascarpone

4 tablespoons ground almonds

4 ripe peaches, pitted and sliced

4 figs, halved or quartered

1 tablespoon dark muscovado sugar, preferably unrefined

Serves 6

Variations:

• Substitute other fruits, such as blueberries and plums, nectarines or poached pears.

1

Grease a 35 x 10 cm tranche tin or 22 cm circular tin and line with a single layer of filo pastry (about 2 overlapping sheets). Trim the pastry leaving about 1 cm sticking up above the rim of the tin. Brush with melted butter and line with another 2 sheets of pastry. Repeat until all the pastry has been used.

2

Beat the sugar and egg in a bowl, then beat in the mascarpone and almonds. Spread over the base of the tart.

3

Arrange the pieces of peaches and figs all over the mascarpone cream until the tart case is full. Sprinkle with the muscovado sugar and brush more butter over the pastry and fruit.

4

Put on a baking sheet and bake on the middle shelf of a preheated oven at 200°C (400°F) Gas 6 for 35 minutes or until tinged golden brown.

Rhubarb and custard pastries

Rhubarb and custard is a favourite combination, but put them on a pastry with a scattering of almonds and you have something downright fabulous. You can cheat a little if you like and buy ready-made custard, but making your own is so easy it's worth trying.

5 stalks young rhubarb, cut into 5 cm lengths

2 tablespoons sugar

1 vanilla pod, split lengthways

300 ml milk

150 ml double cream

4 free-range egg yolks

75 g caster sugar

2 tablespoons plain flour

1 package frozen puff pastry (500 g), thawed

1 tablespoon chopped blanched almonds

icing sugar, for dusting

Serves 6

1

Spread the rhubarb across a wide saucepan in a single layer, sprinkle with the sugar and add about 3 tablespoons water. Heat to simmering, carefully turn over the slices, turn off the heat and cover with a lid – the rhubarb should be poached through and tender. Let cool.

2

Put the split vanilla pod, milk and cream in a saucepan and bring to the boil. Remove from the heat.

3

Beat 3 of the egg yolks, sugar and flour in a bowl until thick and pale. Slowly beat in the hot vanilla milk (discard the pod). Pour the custard back into the milk pan and cook very gently, stirring all the time, for about 1 minute – don't let it boil, or it will curdle. Remove from the heat.

4

Roll out the puff pastry to 5 mm thick and cut into small square shapes or a long rectangle. Spread custard over the top, leaving a 5 mm edge of pastry uncovered. Top with lines of rhubarb, push the nuts into the pastry and brush with the remaining egg yolk, beaten. Dust with icing sugar and bake in a preheated oven at 200°C (400°F) Gas 6 for 20 minutes for small pastries or 30 minutes if large, until puffed and golden.

5

Dust with more icing sugar and serve warm.

Pear tart with Catalan custard

A line of pears put to bed on a puffed blanket of pastry. I've used a thin, *crème-anglaise*-style custard flavoured with citrus peel, as the Spanish do to make *crème catalan*. It can be thickened with 2 teaspoons of cornflour.

1 tablespoon lemon juice

4 unripe pears

1 vanilla pod, split lengthways

125 g caster sugar

400 g fresh, ready-made puff pastry

1 egg, lightly beaten

icing sugar, for dusting

Catalan custard:

300 ml milk

300 ml double cream

2 cinnamon sticks, broken

grated zest of ½ lemon

100 g caster sugar

6 egg yolks

Serves 8

1

Put the milk, cream, cinnamon and lemon in a saucepan and bring to the boil. Remove from the heat and set aside for 30 minutes.

2

Half fill a saucepan with water. Add the lemon juice. Peel the pears and put them straight into the pan to stop browning. Add the vanilla pod and sugar, bring to the boil and simmer for 25 minutes until just tender.

3

Roll out the pastry, 3–5 mm thick, and cut into 2 long strips, each big enough to fit 4 pear halves, side by side with about 1 cm between. Put on a greased baking sheet. Arrange the halved pears across the pastry and, with the tip of a knife, score a shallow cut in the pastry around each pear. Brush all over with beaten egg. Bake in a preheated oven at 200°C (400°F) Gas 6 for 20–30 minutes until puffed and golden.

4

Whisk the sugar and egg yolks together in a bowl. Strain the milk mixture and whisk into the egg mixture. Pour into a saucepan and heat gently, continuously stirring, until you have a thin custard that coats the back of the spoon (too much heat and the custard will curdle).

5

Dust the tart with icing sugar, slice into portions and serve with custard.

Baby apple pies

Pure unadulterated apple. No fancy flavours or hidden extras – apples can make it on their own. Cooked until silky smooth with a few little chunks for texture, then baked inside a buttery crumbly pastry, this is real comfort food.

375 g plain flour

185 g caster sugar, plus extra for dusting

185 g butter, softened

3 medium egg yolks

mascarpone cheese, to serve

Apple filling:

4 large Bramley cooking apples, peeled, cored and chopped

4 tablespoons caster sugar

juice of ½ lemon

Makes about 12

one 12-hole muffin tray

1

Put the flour in a large bowl, make a well in the centre and tip in the sugar. Add the butter and egg yolks. Using a fork, mash the yolks, butter and sugar together, then draw in the flour. Using your hands, mix well, then transfer to a work surface and knead well for about 30 seconds to form a smooth dough (Add a little extra flour if necessary, to form the right consistency. Wrap in clingfilm and chill for 20 minutes.

2

Put the chopped apple in a saucepan with the sugar, lemon juice and 2 tablespoons water and cook to a coarse purée, leaving a few lumps. Taste and add more sugar if you prefer. Cool, then chill.

3

Roll out the pastry to 5 mm thick. Using a biscuit cutter, stamp out 12 circles to line a mini 12-hole muffin tray and 12 smaller circles for lids. Line the moulds with the larger circles of pastry and fill with the apple mixture. Brush the rim of the pastry with water, top with the smaller circles of pastry and gently press the edges together. Trim with a knife to make neat edges. Make 3 small neat holes in the top of each and dust with sugar.

4

Bake in a preheated oven at 190°C (375°F) Gas 5 for 20–25 minutes until golden at the edges. Let cool a little, then remove, dust with a little more sugar and serve with mascarpone.

Blueberry cheesecake

Yes, there's a pastry to make, but it's so easy, and rolling it straight onto the tin stops it tearing. Easy to make and light to eat: the filling is virtually fat free and the pastry base is so thin you can have seconds without worrying about calories. The base and filling hold up well if you want to make it in advance – add the fresh fruit just before serving.

300 g blueberries or bilberries

mint leaves

icing sugar, for dusting

double cream, to serve (optional)

Pastry base:

60 g caster sugar

125 g unsalted butter, softened

1 egg yolk

1 teaspoon grated lemon zest

185 g plain flour, sifted

Cheesecake filling:

375 g low-fat soft cheese, such as Quark

4 eggs, yolks and whites separated

1 teaspoon grated lemon zest

125 g caster sugar

1 tablespoon plain flour

Serves 6–8

1

Butter a 20 cm springform tin and base-line with greaseproof paper.

2

To prepare the pastry base, mix the sugar, butter, egg yolk and lemon zest in a bowl. Add the flour and work to a smooth dough. If it is too sticky, dust with flour, then work in. Chill for 20 minutes.

3

Put the base of the springform tin on the work surface and roll out the pastry on top to approximately 5 mm thickness. Trim around the base with a knife and discard the excess pastry. Assemble the tin and bake in a preheated oven at 150°C (300°F) Gas 2 for 20 minutes until half cooked. Let cool. Reduce the oven heat to 140°C (275°F) Gas 1.

4

To make the cheesecake filling, mix the cheese in a bowl with the egg yolks and lemon zest. Beat the egg whites until stiff, then gradually beat in the sugar and flour. Fold the egg white mixture into the cheese mixture and spoon over the part-cooked pastry base in the tin. Sprinkle with 2 tablespoons of the berries and bake on the middle shelf of the oven for about 1 hour or until firm to the touch. Let cool.

5

To serve, top with a tumbling pile of the remaining fruit, scatter with a few mint leaves, dust with icing sugar and serve with cream, if using.

Passion cake

You wouldn't look twice at a passionfruit – that's if you didn't know what lay within. It looks far from passionate. The flower is extremely distinctive and this gives rise to its name, symbolizing the Passion of Christ. But the plainest of fruits contains within its hallowed skin a richly perfumed nectar-like mass of juices and seeds (which are edible too). Truly humble on the outside and full of divine things within – halve, scoop out the contents and enjoy.

110 g ground almonds

60 g plain flour, sifted

a pinch of salt

4 eggs, separated

1 vanilla pod, split lengthways

130 g caster sugar

sieved flesh and juice of 6 passionfruit

2 tablespoons icing sugar

Passionfruit syrup:

flesh and seeds of 8 passionfruit

juice of ½ lemon

80 g caster sugar

thick double cream or crème fraîche, to serve

Makes 8 individual heart-shaped cakes

eight 10-cm heart-shaped cake tins, greased and base-lined

1

Mix the ground almonds in a bowl with the flour and salt, and make a well in the centre. In a second bowl, beat the egg yolks and sugar until the mixture is pale and leaves a trail when lifted. Scrape the seeds from the vanilla pod into the mixture and beat well. Stir into the almond mixture, followed by the passionfruit juice.

2

Beat the egg whites to soft peak stage and fold into the cake mixture. Divide between 8 greased and base-lined 10-cm heart-shaped tins and bake in a preheated oven at 180°C (350°F) Gas 4 for about 15–20 minutes until the cake springs back when lightly pressed. Turn out onto a wire rack. Let cool.

3

Put all the syrup ingredients in a saucepan and heat to make a thin syrup. Dust the cakes with icing sugar and serve in a pool of syrup with cream or créme fraîche.

Variation:

• Make a large cake, cool and slice into 3 layers. Fill each layer with mascarpone flavoured with lemon curd.

Hazelnut tiramisu cake

For an alternative topping, melt 250 g dark chocolate with 125 ml double cream and let cool. Beat until thick, then spread the mixture over the top and sides of cake, swirling it into a pattern and decorate with toasted hazelnuts.

4 eggs

250 g caster sugar

190 g plain flour, sieved

100 g hazelnuts, roasted, skinned and coarsely ground

1 teaspoon vanilla essence

Tiramisu filling:

2 eggs

2 tablespoons caster sugar

650 g mascarpone

250 ml double cream

120 ml strong coffee (cold)

4 tablespoons coffee liqueur, such as Kahlua

cocoa powder, for dusting

Chocolate band (optional):*

300 g dark chocolate (at least 70% cocoa solids), broken into pieces

Serves 4–6

2 round 18-cm springform cake tins, buttered and base-lined with baking parchment.

1

To make the cake, whisk the eggs with an electric whisk or mixer until frothy. Gradually whisk in the sugar until the mixture is absolutely white and holds its shape. Fold in the flour, hazelnuts and vanilla. Divide the mixture between the cake tins. Bake in a preheated oven at 180°C (350°F) Gas 4 for 25–30 minutes, or until firm to the touch. Let cool, then remove the paper and slice each sponge into 2 rounds.

2

To make the filling, beat the eggs with the sugar in a large bowl, then beat in the mascarpone. Reserve one-third of the mixture in a small bowl. Beat the cream to soft peak stage and fold into the mixture in the large bowl. Mix the coffee with the coffee liqueur in a cup or small jug.

3

To assemble the cake, put a round of sponge on a serving plate and sprinkle with the liqueur coffee mixture. Cover with a thick layer of mascarpone cream. Top with another round of sponge and repeat the process until all the sponge has been used. (Don't sprinkle coffee right to the edges and leave the top sponge unsprinkled.) Using a palette knife, cover the top and sides of the cake with the reserved mascarpone. Add the chocolate band (see note). Chill. Dust with cocoa powder if you like.

__Note:__ To make the Chocolate Band, melt the chocolate in a heatproof bowl set over a pan of simmering water until smooth and lump-free. Cut out a rectangle of acetate (from art shops) measuring the circumference x height of the assembled cake. Set on a smooth work surface. Pour the mixture over the acetate, spreading with a palette knife until the edges are covered. Smooth level. Let cool until almost set, but still pliable. Lift up the acetate band and bend it around the cake (chocolate on the inside) with a small overlapping 'seam' and secure with tape. Refrigerate until set, then remove the tape and carefully peel off the acetate.

Nut fudge shortbread

Caramel squares, found in old-fashioned bakers, cafés and tea shops, are pretty lethal. Sweetly addictive, they will work wonders (but in the wrong direction – to your waistline). Eat one, do eighty press-ups, that's the way to do it. I make mine with nuts and raisins.

300 g plain flour

a pinch of salt

120 g caster sugar

240 g unsalted butter

200 g plump raisins

220 g pecans or walnut halves

200 g dark chocolate

Fudge:

120 g unsalted butter

120 g light muscovado sugar

2 tablespoons golden syrup

170 g sweetened condensed milk (1 small can)

Serves 4–6

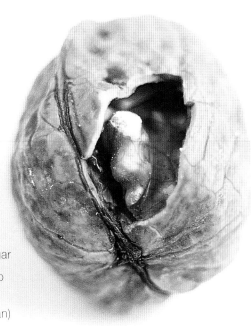

1

To make the shortbread, put the flour, salt, sugar and butter into a food processor and pulse until the pastry forms a ball. Alternatively, using your fingertips, rub the butter into the flour to resemble fine crumbs, then work in the salt and sugar. Press the mixture into a 20 x 30 cm Swiss roll tin. Sprinkle with raisins and press flat. Bake in a preheated oven at 180°C (350°F) Gas 4 for 25–30 minutes or until golden.

2

Put all the fudge ingredients into a non-stick saucepan and heat gently, but do not boil. Whisk thoroughly together.

3

Line the nuts across the cooked shortbread base, then pour over the hot fudge mixture. Smooth with a palette knife and chill until firm.

4

Melt the chocolate in a heatproof bowl set over a saucepan of gently simmering water. Pour the chocolate over the set fudge mixture, smooth with a palette knife and leave to set. Cut into slices or fingers before serving.

index

A

allspice cabbage with shallots and sausages, 140

almonds: peach and fig almond tart, 159
Persian chicken with coconut and almonds, 102

anise braised pork with Chinese mustard cabbage, 135

apples: baby apple pies, 165
caramel syrup apples, 148
pecan pork with apple and maple syrup, 137
pot-roasted game bird with apple, cabbage, juniper and cream, 116

Asian greens, asparagus soup with, 11

asparagus: asparagus brunch with prosciutto soldiers, 22
asparagus filo tart with spinach and potato, 45
asparagus soup with Asian greens, 11
salmon fish fingers with asparagus, spring pods and mustard-mint butter, 88

aubergines: aubergine croutons, 16
aubergine mozzarella lasagne, 48
baba ganoush, 127
Indian spiced aubergine, 60–1
lamb burgers with char-grilled aubergine, hoummus, seed salt and mint, 127
prawn and pea aubergine laksa, 75

avocado and coriander toast, 28

B

baba ganoush, 127

bacon: bacon-wrapped monkfish with Brussels tops, 85
pea quiche, 32

basil oil, spinach gnocchi with, 50

beans: roasted vine tomatoes with cannellini bean salad, 38

beef: beef stew with chestnuts, 122
pub beef and onion pies, 124

beer batter, rock salmon in, 87

bhajia, corn and sweet potato, 55

blackened salmon with oven-roasted tomato salad, 80

blistered peaches with chilli kaffir lime ice, 151

blueberry cheesecake, 166

bread: Christmas turkey for two with bread sauce stuffing, 115
honeyed duck with baby chard, coriander and mustard seed mayo in ciabatta, 108
roasted tomatoes in herb oil with char-grilled bread, 24–5

broad beans: broad bean felafels, 41
Parma chicken kiev with peas and, 101

Brussels sprouts, Christmas turkey for two with bread sauce stuffing and, 115

Brussels tops, bacon-wrapped monkfish with, 85

butter beans: rosemary and olive lamb with roasted garlic butter beans, 128

butternut squash: grilled chicken and pumpkin couscous, 98

C

cabbage: allspice cabbage with shallots and sausages, 140
pot-roasted game bird with apple, cabbage, juniper and cream, 116

Caesar greens with gentleman's relish toast, 36

cakes: hazelnut tiramisu cake, 171
passion cake, 168

cannellini bean salad, roasted vine tomatoes with, 38

caramel syrup apples, 148

Catalan custard, pear tart with, 162

celeriac: pastrami salmon with caraway celeriac, 78

chard: honeyed duck with baby chard, coriander and mustard seed mayo in ciabatta, 108

cheese: aubergine mozzarella lasagne, 48
Indian coconut dhaal with peas and paneer, 52
porcini pizza with garlic butter, 67
pot-roasted red onions with feta cheese and oregano, 62
roasted mushrooms with horseradish mascarpone, 30
roasted tomatoes in herb oil with baby mozzarella, 24–5
rosewater-poached rhubarb with vanilla ricotta, 146
spinach gnocchi with basil oil, 50
summer lasagne, 46

cheesecake, blueberry, 166

chestnuts, beef stew with, 122

chicken, 92–106
chicken and butter leek soup, 13
chicken and mushroom pie, 106
chicken and pea shoot salad, 95
grilled chicken and pumpkin couscous, 98
mango lapsang chicken and herb salad, 97
Parma chicken kiev with peas, broad beans, mint and basil, 101
Persian chicken with coconut and almonds, 102

chickpeas: broad bean felafels, 41

chillies: chilli crisp prawns and garlic chives, 71
chilli kaffir lime ice, 151
kumquat duck with chilli citrus sauce, 110
sambal dips, 55

Chinese mustard cabbage, anise braised pork with, 135

chocolate: hazelnut tiramisu cake, 171
nut fudge shortbread, 172

chowder, Jerusalem artichoke, 18

Christmas turkey for two, 115

clay pot lemon poussin, 104

coconut milk: Indian coconut dhaal, 52
Persian chicken with coconut and almonds, 102
pumpkin coconut curry, 59

coffee: hazelnut tiramisu cake, 171

coriander: avocado and coriander toast, 28

corn cobs: corn and sweet potato bhajia with sambal dip, 55
seafood and corn gumbo, 73

courgettes: summer lasagne, 46

couscous: grilled chicken and pumpkin couscous, 98

curries: green tomato and basil curry, 56
prawn and pea aubergine laksa, 75
pumpkin coconut curry, 59

custard: pear tart with Catalan custard, 162
rhubarb and custard pastries, 160

D

duck: honeyed duck with baby chard, coriander and mustard seed mayo in ciabatta, 108
kumquat duck with chilli citrus sauce, 110
root and honey duck hot pot, 113

E

eggs: asparagus brunch with prosciutto soldiers, 22
Indian spiced aubergine with egg, basil and cardamom rice, 60–1

F

felafels, broad bean, 41

figs: peach and fig almond tart, 159

fish and seafood, 68–91

fish fingers, salmon, 88

fishcakes: smoked fishcakes with lemon butter spinach, 90

fruit: green fruit gado gado with lime and peanut dressing, 26
summer pudding toast, 157

fudge: nut fudge shortbread, 172

G

gado gado, green fruit, 26

game bird, pot-roasted, 116

garlic: porcini pizza with garlic butter, 67
rosemary and olive lamb with roasted garlic butter beans, 128

garlic chives, chilli crisp prawns and, 71

gentleman's relish toast, Caesar greens with, 36

ginger toffee pears with rice pudding, 152

gnocchi: spinach gnocchi with basil oil, 50

goats' cheese, pumpkin soup with Creole roasted pumpkin seeds and, 14

green fruit gado gado, 26

green tomato and basil curry, 56

greens: Caesar greens with gentleman's relish toast, 36
pot-roasted game bird with apple, cabbage, juniper and cream, 116

H

ham and peas, 139

hazelnut tiramisu cake, 171

honeyed duck, 108

horseradish picada, bacon-wrapped monkfish with, 85
roasted mushrooms with horseradish mascarpone, 30
thyme buttered baby roots with home-made horseradish cream, 64

hot water crust pastry, 124

I

ice cream: chilli kaffir lime ice, 151
raspberry ripple, 144

Indian coconut dhaal, 52

Indian spiced aubergine, 60–1

J

Jerusalem artichoke chowder with pan-seared scallops, 18

K

kaffir limes: chilli kaffir lime ice, 151

kumquat duck with chilli citrus sauce, 110

L

lamb: lamb burgers with char-grilled aubergine, 127
lamb shanks with autumn squash ratatouille, 130
rosemary and olive lamb, 128

lasagne: aubergine mozzarella lasagne, 48
summer lasagne, 46

leeks: chicken and butter leek soup, 13

lemon: clay pot lemon poussin, 104
lemon herb-cured salmon trout, 76

lemongrass yoghurt rice, 154

limes: chilli kaffir lime ice, 151

M

mangetout: steamed sea bass with soy beans and, 82

mango lapsang chicken and herb salad, 97

meat, 120–41

monkfish, bacon-wrapped, 85

morels: chicken and mushroom pie, 106

mushrooms: chicken and mushroom pie, 106
porcini pizza with garlic butter, 67
pork chops with peppered wild mushroom gravy, 132
roasted mushrooms with horseradish mascarpone, 30

N

noodles: prawn and pea aubergine laksa, 75

　spice island noodle soup, 20

nut fudge shortbread, 172

O

okra: seafood and corn gumbo, 73

olives: lamb shanks with autumn squash ratatouille, 130

　rosemary and olive lamb, 128

onions: pot-roasted red onions, 62

　pub beef and onion pies, 124

oranges: kumquat duck with chilli citrus sauce, 110

P

paneer, Indian coconut dhaal with peas and, 52

Parma chicken kiev, 101

passion cake, 168

pastrami salmon with caraway celeriac, 78

pastries, rhubarb and custard, 160

　see also pies; tarts

pastry, hot water crust, 124

pea shoots: chicken and pea shoot salad, 95

peaches: blistered peaches with chilli kaffir lime ice, 151

　peach and fig almond tart, 159

　squab and peach tagine, 119

peanuts: green fruit gado gado with lime and peanut dressing, 26

pears: ginger toffee pears, 152

　pear tart with Catalan custard, 162

peas: ham and peas, 139

　Indian coconut dhaal with paneer and, 52

　Parma chicken kiev with, 101

　pea quiche, 32

　rock salmon in beer batter with pease pudding, 87

peas, yellow split: Indian coconut dhaal, 52

pecan nuts: nut fudge shortbread, 172

　pecan pork with apple and maple syrup, 137

peppers: lamb shanks with autumn squash ratatouille, 130

　tomato and pepper soup, 16

Persian chicken with coconut and almonds, 102

pies: baby apple pies, 165

　chicken and mushroom pie, 106

　pub beef and onion pies, 124

pigeon: squab and peach tagine, 119

pimientos: tomato and pimiento tart, 42

pizzas: porcini pizza with garlic butter, 67

porcini pizza with garlic butter, 67

pork: anise braised pork with Chinese mustard cabbage, 135

　pecan pork with apple and maple syrup, 137

pork chops with peppered wild mushroom gravy, 132

spice island noodle soup, 20

potatoes: asparagus filo tart with spinach and, 45

　lemon herb-cured salmon trout with dill potatoes, 76

　smoked fishcakes, 90

poussin, clay pot lemon, 104

prawns: chilli crisp prawns and garlic chives, 71

　prawn and pea aubergine laksa, 75

　spice island noodle soup, 20

prosciutto soldiers, asparagus brunch with, 22

pub beef and onion pies, 124

puddings, 142–72

pumpkin: grilled chicken and pumpkin couscous, 98

　pumpkin coconut curry, 59

　pumpkin soup with Creole roasted pumpkin seeds, 14

Q

quiche, pea, 32

R

raisins: nut fudge shortbread, 172

raspberries: lemongrass yoghurt rice with crushed raspberries, 154

　raspberry ripple, 144

ratatouille: lamb shanks with autumn squash ratatouille, 130

rhubarb: rhubarb and custard pastries, 160

　rosewater-poached rhubarb with vanilla ricotta, 146

rice: ginger toffee pears with rice pudding, 152

　Indian spiced aubergine with egg, basil and cardamom rice, 60-1

　lemongrass yoghurt rice, 154

rock salmon in beer batter, 87

root vegetables: root and honey duck hot pot, 113

　thyme buttered baby roots, 64

rosemary and olive lamb, 128

rosewater-poached rhubarb, 146

S

salads: blackened salmon with oven-roasted tomato salad, 80

　chicken and pea shoot salad, 95

　dill potato salad, 76

　green fruit gado gado, 26

　herb radish salad, 41

　mango lapsang chicken and herb salad, 97

　roasted vine tomatoes with cannellini bean salad, 38

salmon: blackened salmon, 80

　pastrami salmon with caraway celeriac, 78

rock salmon in beer batter, 87

　salmon fish fingers, 88

salmon trout, lemon herb-cured, 76

sambal dip, 55

sausages, allspice cabbage with shallots and, 140

scallops: Jerusalem artichoke chowder with pan-seared scallops, 18

sea bass: steamed sea bass with mangetout and soy beans, 82

seafood, 68–91

seafood and corn gumbo, 73

shortbread, nut fudge, 172

smoked fishcakes with lemon butter spinach, 90

smoking chicken, 97

soups, 8–20

　asparagus soup with Asian greens, 11

　chicken and butter leek soup, 13

　Jerusalem artichoke chowder, 18

pumpkin soup with Creole roasted pumpkin seeds, 14

　spice island noodle soup, 20

　tomato and pepper soup, 16

soy beans, steamed sea bass with mangetout and, 82

spaghetti squash: pumpkin coconut curry, 59

spice island noodle soup, 20

spinach: asparagus filo tart with potato and, 45

　smoked fishcakes with lemon butter spinach, 90

　spinach gnocchi with basil oil, 50

squab and peach tagine, 119

squash: grilled chicken and pumpkin couscous, 98

　lamb shanks with autumn squash ratatouille, 130

summer lasagne, 46

summer pudding toast, 157

sweet potatoes: corn and sweet potato bhajia, 55

T

tagine, squab and peach, 119

tarts: asparagus filo tart, 45

　peach and fig almond tart, 159

　pear tart with Catalan custard, 162

　tomato and pimiento tart, 42

thyme buttered baby roots, 64

tiramisu cake, hazelnut, 171

toast: avocado and coriander toast, 28

　Caesar greens with gentleman's relish toast, 36

　roasted mushrooms with horseradish mascarpone, 30

　summer pudding toast, 157

toffee: ginger toffee pears, 152

tomatoes: blackened salmon with oven-roasted tomato salad, 80

　green tomato and basil curry, 56

　roasted tomatoes in herb oil, 24-5

　roasted vine tomatoes with cannellini bean salad, 38

　sambal dips, 55

　summer lasagne, 46

　tomato and pepper soup, 16

　tomato and pimiento tart, 42

turkey: Christmas turkey for two, 115

V

vegetables, 34–67

　root and honey duck hot pot, 113

　thyme buttered baby roots, 64

W

water spinach: asparagus soup with Asian greens, 11

Y

yoghurt: lemongrass yoghurt rice, 154

Acknowledgements

My thanks to Egg, of Kinnerton Street, Belgravia, London, who were so generous in lending beautiful bowls for photography, and Kara Kara, of Tokyo and Pond Place, South Kensington in London, for Japanese ceramics and other props; to the Conran Shop, Fulham Road, London, for the white ceramic platters. Thanks also to City Herbs of New Spitalfield Market, London and Panzas, 19 Circus Road, London NW8 for great fruit and vegetables. Finally, many thanks to Halcyon Herbs for the salad leaves and herbs. They sell seeds by mail order from 10 Hampden Close, Chalgrove, Oxford, OX44 7SB, England. Fax 01865 890 180.